New Zealand Bird Views

TERNS

Raewyn Adams

Published 2012
Te Puke, New Zealand.
© Text and photos Raewyn Adams
The author asserts her moral right to be identified as the author of this work.

ISBN 978-0-473-20174-6

Copies of this book can be purchased from www.lulu.com
Author contact radams.photo@gmail.com

Front cover: White-fronted tern. Tauranga Harbour.

CONTENTS

SERIES INTRODUCTION

The concept of this series is to present and appreciate the birds that people are likely to view around them. These are the common birds that are around us every day but we fail to really see because they are always just "there".

The intent of this series is to tell the bird's story in photos. In this format the reader can see more of the bird's life and gain an understanding and appreciation of its place in nature and how it interacts with the world it lives in – its relationships with other birds, the environment and also with people.

When you get to know them, birds are fascinating animals. They have complex social structures, sophisticated communication systems and are very hard workers. They are also very beautiful. The feathers of even the plainest birds have amazing textures and intricate patterns.

I have provided some basic factual information. For those wanting more depth there is a starting point in the list of further information resources at the end of the book. The rest of the book consists of my personal observations, illustrated with photographs as much as possible.

I hope you enjoy these views of the birds around us.

TERNS IN NEW ZEALAND

Three species of tern are commonly seen in New Zealand:

- **Black-fronted terns** (*Sterna albostriata*) breed in the braided rivers of the South Island and move northwards and towards the coast in winter. There are about 7,000-10,000 birds. Size 290mm. Endemic.

- **Caspian terns** (*Sterna caspia*) live mainly near the coast all year but may also occasionally be seen near inland waterways. They are more abundant in northern areas. There are about 50,000 pairs found in temperate areas throughout the world, with about 3,000 pairs in New Zealand. Size 510mm. Native.

- **White-fronted terns** (*Sterna striata*) are birds of the seashore and harbours and up to 20,000 pairs breed throughout New Zealand's coastline. During the winter many migrate to Australia but large numbers also remain in New Zealand and congregate in colonies near the sea. Size 400mm. Endemic.

These three species are the terns most commonly seen, but others may also be found from time to time. The fairy tern is another endemic species and is highly endangered. Other terns migrating from northern to southern locations may stray on to the New Zealand mainland. I have listed these at the end of the book.

The different species have similarities but are also quite different from one another. Each has unique needs but their habitats do overlap from time to time.

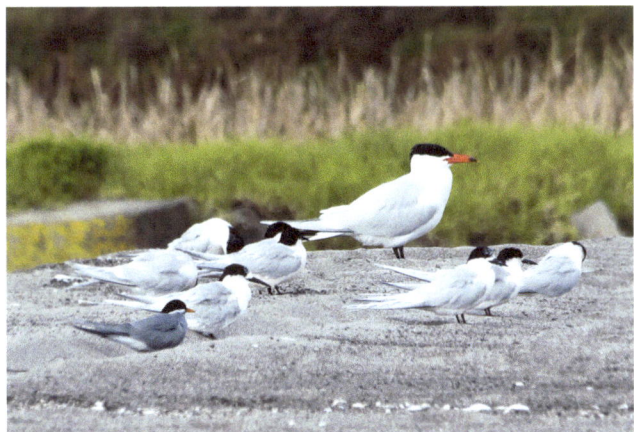

All three species together – showing the relative size of each. Caspian tern at rear. Black-fronted tern front left. The others are white-fronted terns. Initially the Caspian tern was resting about 20 metres away from the main flock of terns. The flock took to the air then landed coincidentally next to the Caspian tern, which moved away a few minutes later. Thornton, Bay of Plenty. July.

In spite of their differences there seems to be a recognition of a kind as the different species will mix when they meet, although this does have limitations.

The Caspian terns I have seen near white-fronted terns have been a few metres away from the main group of white-fronted terns. The day that I saw all three of the common species together, the four black-fronted terns flew with the flock of white-fronted terns but when the birds were roosting they stayed together on the edge of the group.

Terns are usually recognisable as terns. They have similarities of body shape and colouration that are fairly clear. The three species shown here are easily identifiable by body size, wing colour and bill colour. Some other species are not so obvious, especially when seasonal and juvenile variations are considered.

It is always worth checking a group of terns for "odd" birds that may be a less common species joining in with the flock. Such birds are often migratory vagrants that have gone off course for some reason. These birds can appear anywhere at any time, but are only seen occasionally.

Similarity between terns and gulls is very superficial. Terns have similar colouration to red-billed or black-billed gulls but most terns have a black or dark head. New Zealand gulls always have a white head. Gulls also have a very different body shape. Even in flight the difference between terns and gulls is easily seen.

The black-fronted, white-fronted and Caspian terns may all seem to be common enough to not be ser-iously endangered, but, as with many other birds today, suitable nest sites are reducing as man impacts more and more on the natural environment.

Many terns nest in a simple unlined hollow in sand or shingle. This is called a scrape and without any protection it is vulnerable to destruction by dogs, feral animals, vehicles and people on foot. Some birds choose other nest locations such as rocky cliffs, harbour piles or bridge structures. These may also be dangerous in ways the birds don't understand if they are too close people, dogs, vehicles, etc.

Terns are not overly fearful of people but, unlike gulls, they don't see us as a source of food and therefore have no need to engage with us. Gulls will look for food anywhere, but terns catch their own live food and therefore don't need people.

Because they rely on live food caught from the sea, white-fronted and Caspian terns are usually seen flying over water rather than land.

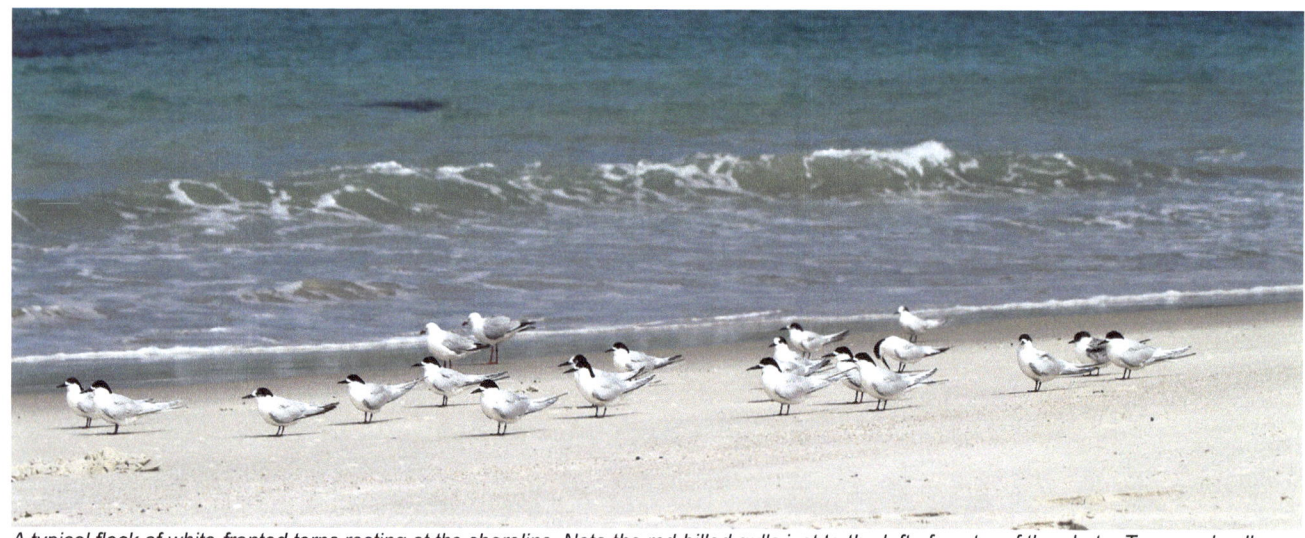

A typical flock of white-fronted terns resting at the shoreline. Note the red-billed gulls just to the left of centre of the photo. Terns and gulls often rest near one another. Kapowairua, Far North. November.

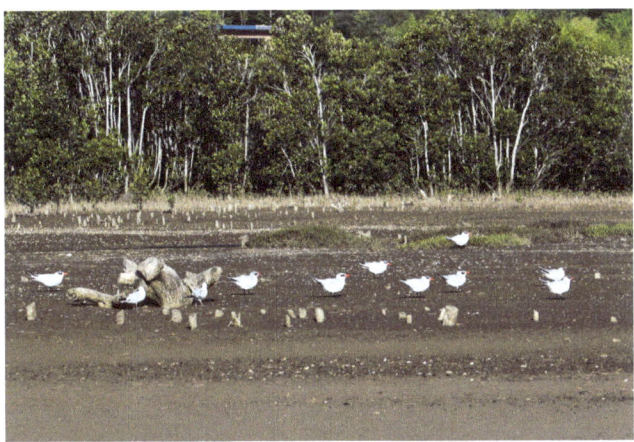

Typical habitat – a group of nine Caspian terns and two red-billed gulls resting in a small river estuary. They roosted on the estuary side of the spit and bathed in the fresh water, but were not far from the outlet to the ocean. Tauranga Bay, Northland. April.

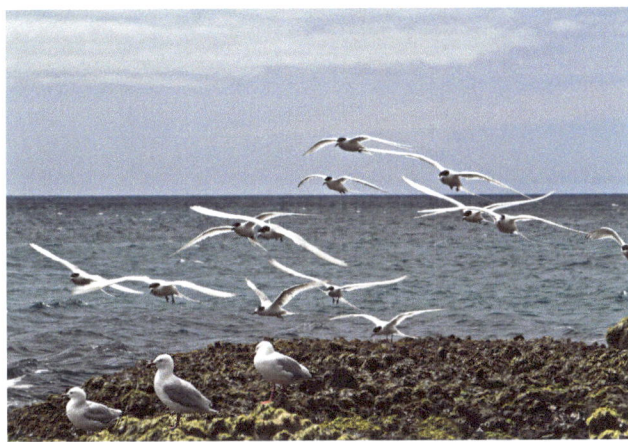

Another typical habitat - a rocky outcrop. The red-billed gulls were already settled when the flock of white-fronted terns flew in and landed among them. They were comfortable roosting together. Kapowairua, Far North. November.

Moving together - a group of white-fronted and black-fronted terns coming in to land on the sand bar between harbour and ocean. Thornton, Bay of Plenty. July

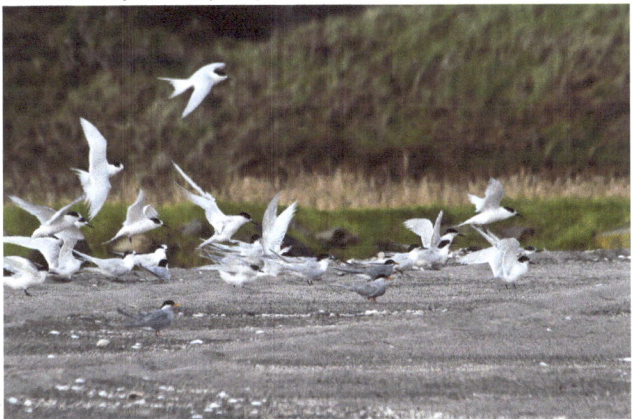

White-fronted terns resting on wet sand in the late afternoon. Even when there is little wind to face into they still all stand facing the same direction. Kapowairua, Far North. November.

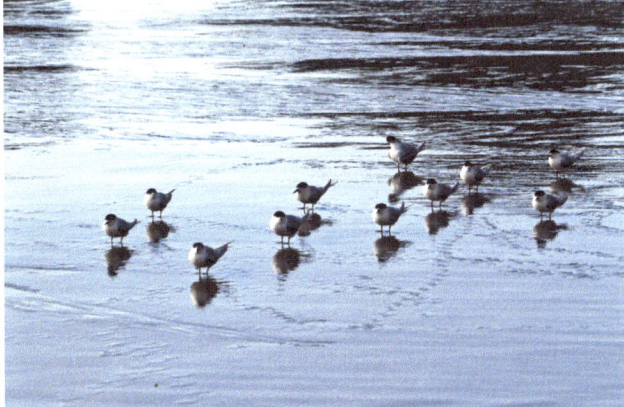

BLACK-FRONTED TERNS

Black-fronted terns are the smallest of the three terns commonly seen. They are found in the rivers of the Canterbury region from October to December - their breeding season. During the winter they move towards coastal areas and are also found further north.

They are often seen near white-fronted terns. Those in the photos were together in a small group on the outer edge of the group of white-fronted terns. I approached them quietly and they were more relaxed about my

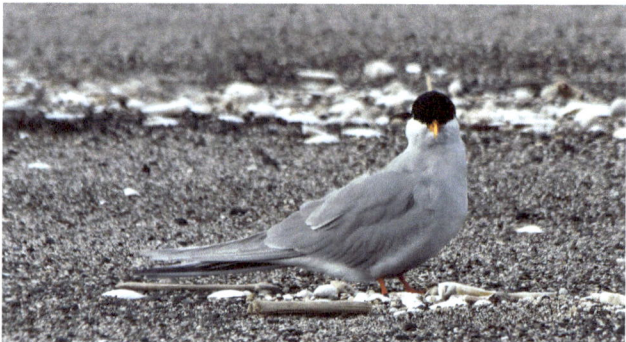

Adult black-fronted tern. Thornton, Bay of Plenty. July.

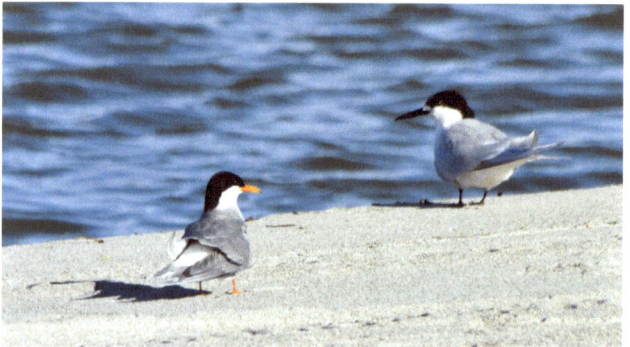

Back view of a black-fronted tern - its feathers ruffled in the wind. Thornton, Bay of Plenty. July.

presence than some of the white-fronted terns that were further away from me. But of course they also had limits about how close I could come.

The black-fronted terns are a darker grey than white-fronted and Caspian terns. This colour helps them to hide among river stones. With an orange bill and legs they are overall a very attractive little bird.

When nesting they live in groups of up to 50 pairs. When dispersed in winter, some flocks may be up to 200-300 birds. There will also be smaller flocks and a few stragglers go as far north as the Bay of Plenty.

Their food may include small fish and marine crustaceans, especially in winter, but is usually more insect-based – either aquatic insects taken from the surface of the water or by hawking flying insects. They will also feed on earthworms, skinks, cicadas and beetle larvae taken from the soil surface.

The nest sites in the gravel of the braided rivers are vulnerable to flooding and may be run over by vehicles or attacked by predators. There is also further risk because of changing environments caused by activities like irrigation schemes or changes in habitat when plants such as lupins and gorse take over.

Nests that are disturbed by people are initially vigorously defended and may be abandoned if there is too much disturbance. Chicks leave the nest almost as soon as they hatch and after a few days start to roam throughout their environment and are able to swim. At about four weeks old they fledge and start feeding themselves, although the parents continue to feed and care for them for several more weeks.

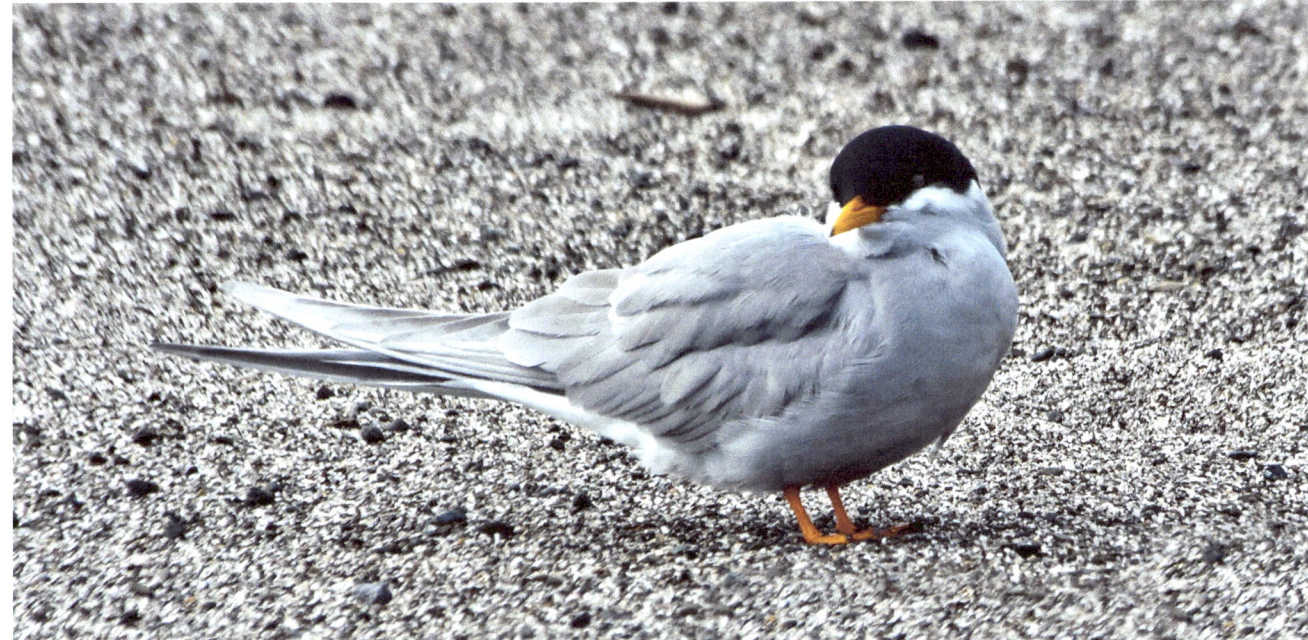

Adult black-fronted tern. Thornton, Bay of Plenty. July.

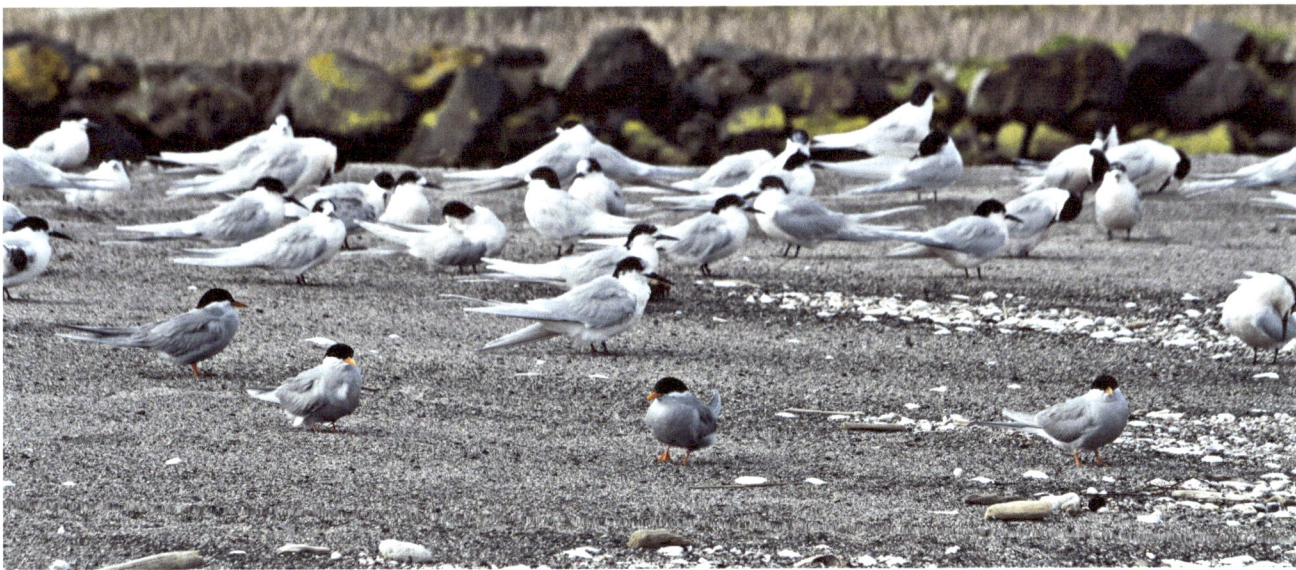

Four black-fronted terns (foreground) resting adjacent to a flock of white-fronted terns. Thornton, Bay of Plenty. July.

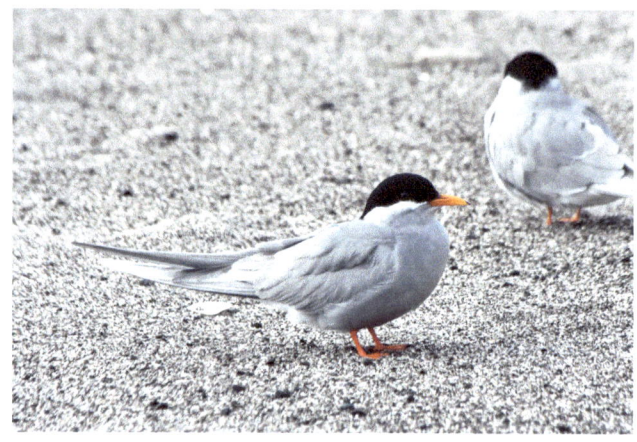
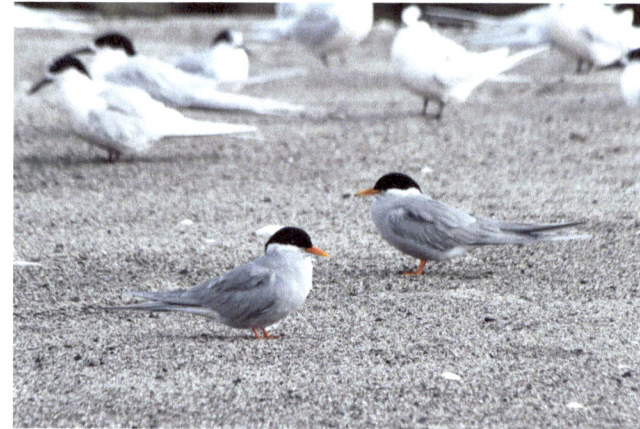

Adult black-fronted terns. Thornton, Bay of Plenty. July.

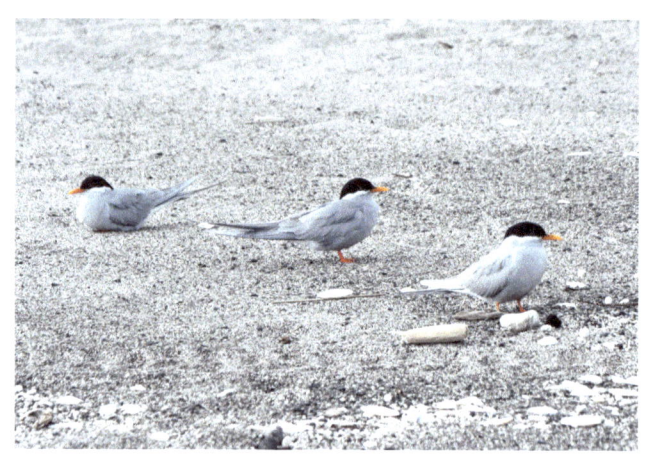
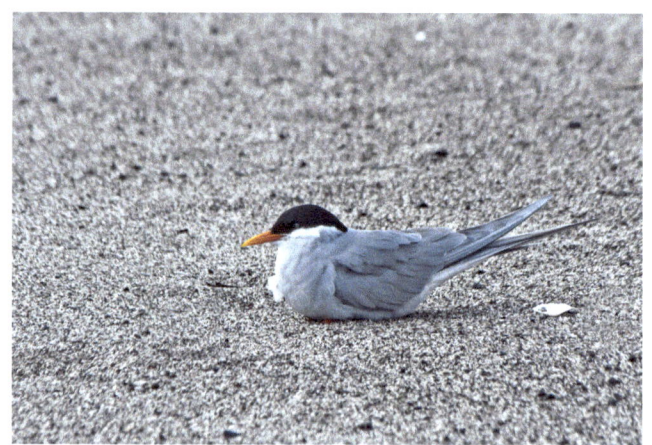

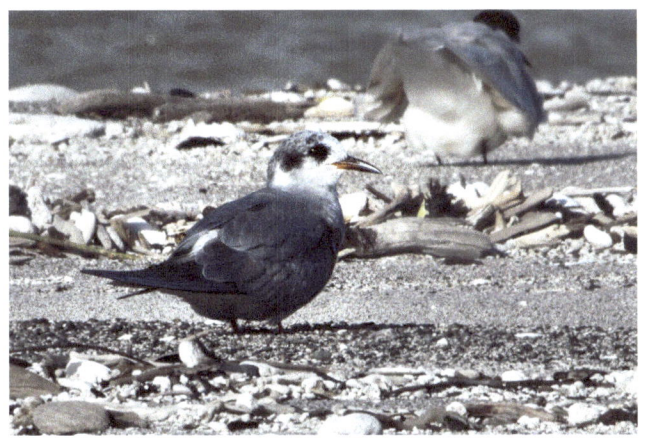

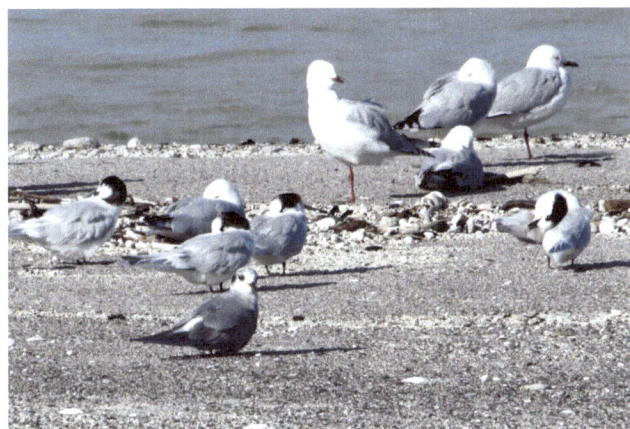

This lone juvenile black-fronted tern roosted with a flock of white-fronted terns and red-billed gulls. Thornton, Bay of Plenty. April.

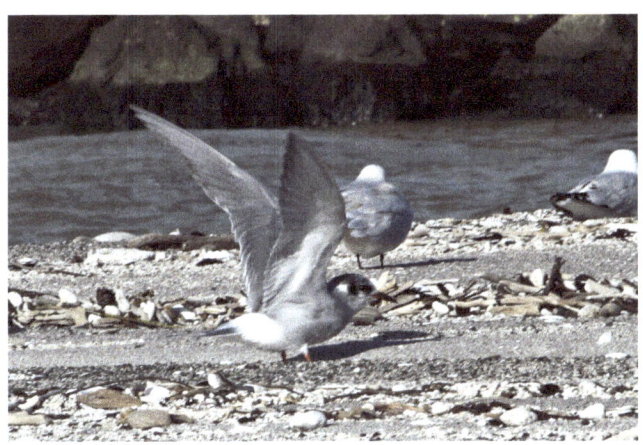

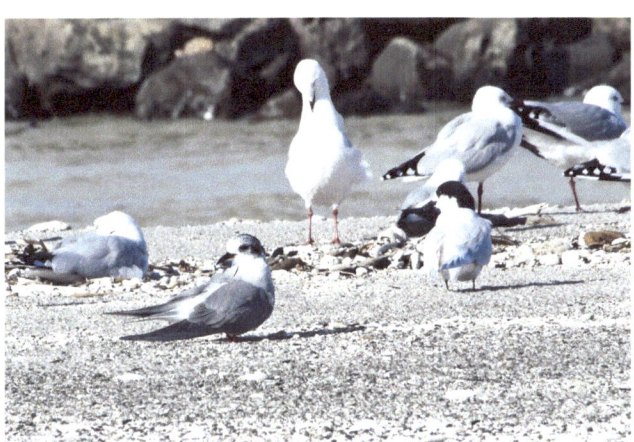

CASPIAN TERNS

Caspian terns are the largest terns. They are most likely to be found resting in small groups or even alone, although large flocks may form in some areas. They may be seen near groups of white-fronted terns, but are usually a little apart from the group rather than within it. The large red bill with a black tip is the key feature to watch for, as well as the large size.

Caspian terns have a stocky build with squat posture when resting. The body looks quite long compared to the short legs and the overall impression is of a fairly scruffy bird.

They were first seen in New Zealand about the 1860s and over time became more common. Threats from habitat disturbance caused by human activities have caused a decline in numbers in recent years. Because they self-introduced they are considered native birds and are therefore protected.

Although Caspian terns are often found near white-fronted terns, they are not as abundant. They may be found on any open beach and are often on the sand bar between a river and its opening to the sea. The Caspian terns may also be found resting or bathing on the estuary side of the sand bar. White-fronted terns are more likely to rest on the seaward side, or at the point where the two bodies of water meet.

When seen in groups, the individual Caspian terns will often be more spread out than groups of other terns. They seem to have a greater requirement for individual space. Possibly this is because when they are resting in small groups they feel less secure than if they were in a large group.

This need for individual space is also apparent when the birds are approached. While not being overly concerned at the presence of people, the distance at which they start to show discomfort and move away is further than that for white-fronted or black-fronted terns.

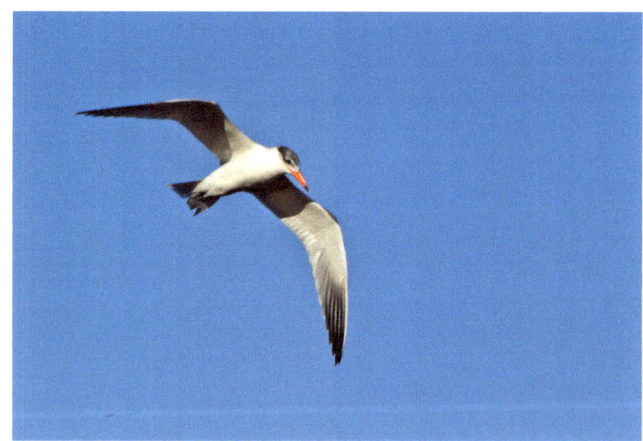

Caspian tern in a typical beach front stance. It's body looks long and its legs short. Rangiputa, Northland. April.

Caspian tern in flight. Matata, Bay of Plenty. July.

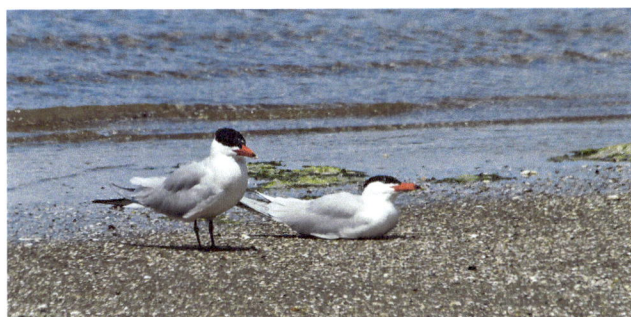

Caspian terns at rest. The bird at the right has tilted its head to take a better look at me. Waikareao Estuary, Tauranga. November.

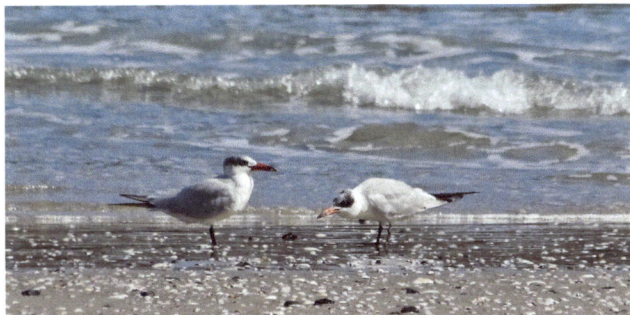

Adult (left) and juvenile Caspian terns. The young bird is in the typical "begging for food" stance. Kapowairua, Far North. April.

Caspian terns breed in single pairs and small colonies on sandy beaches, estuaries and harbours. After breeding they move around New Zealand to a degree, but often stay fairly close to their nest site. North Island birds range up to 100km. South Island birds travel further, with some coming to the North Island.

The nest sites on bare sandspits are vulnerable to damage by human and predator activity. Breeding birds may tolerate people near the nest while they are sitting on eggs, but disturbance of young should be

avoided. The parents are not afraid to attack if they feel threatened.

Young birds will continue to follow a parent and beg for food for several months. The young bird follows the parent wherever it goes, and whines incessantly for food.

Caspian terns eat only fish and have a life span of more than 20 years.

The variable oystercatchers walking past the Caspian tern show that the tern is a similar size to them - a lot larger than other terns. Thornton, Bay of Plenty. July.

Immature and adult Caspian terns on a rocky shore. Hihi, Northland. April.

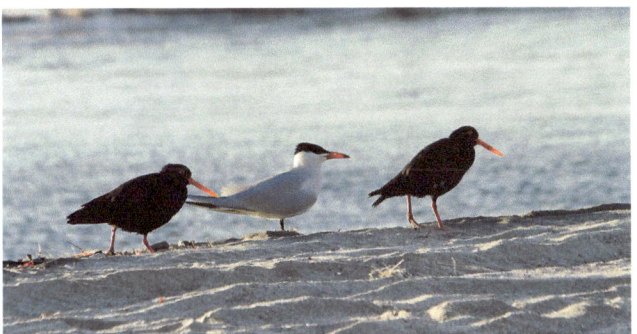

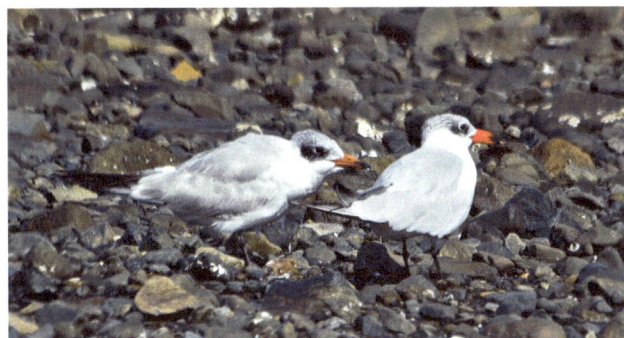

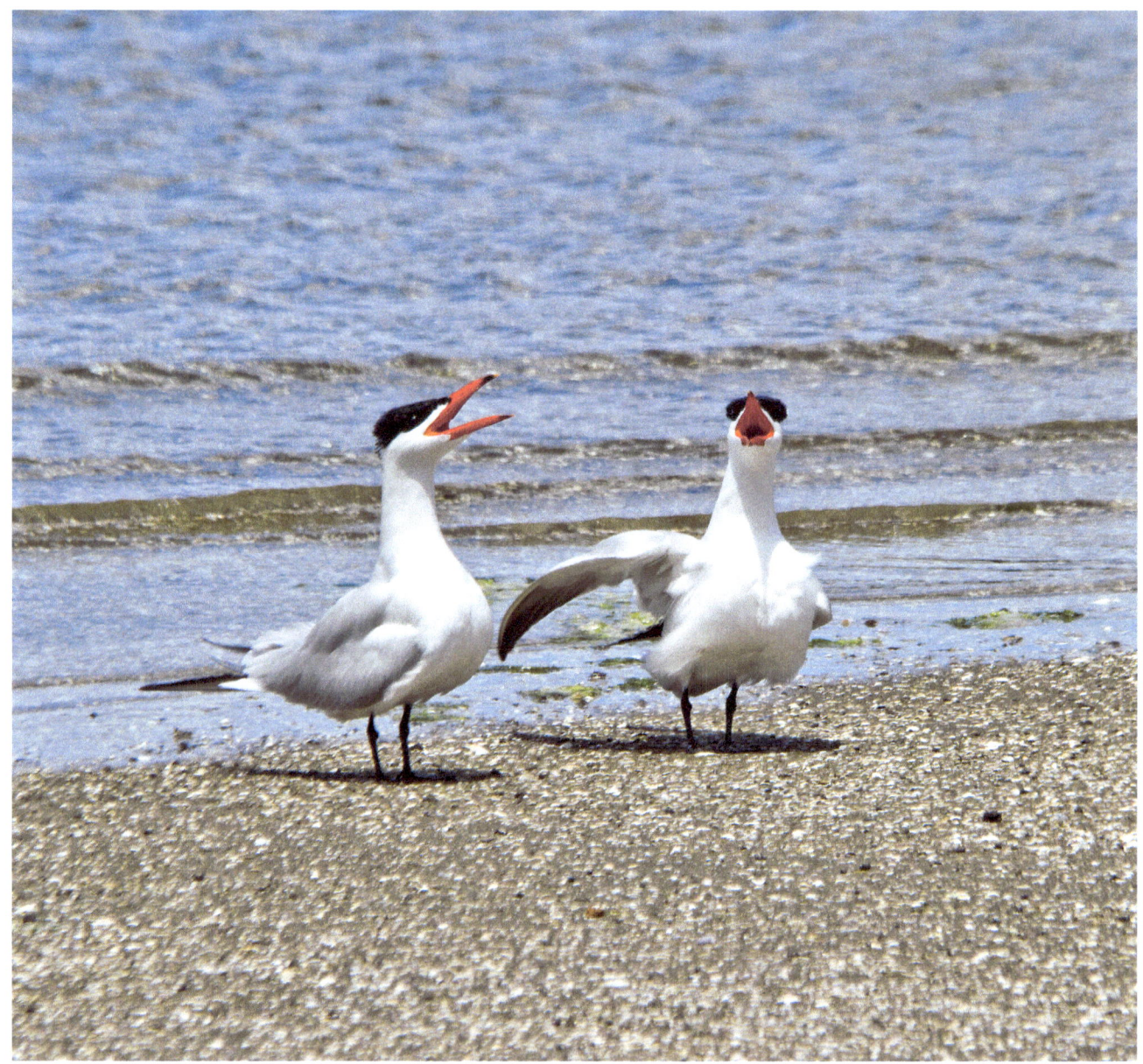

A pair of Caspian terns resting on the shoreline. The closer bird was more aggressive so was presumably the male. He raised his head and barked at me several times. This time his mate joined in too. Waikareao Estuary, Tauranga. November.

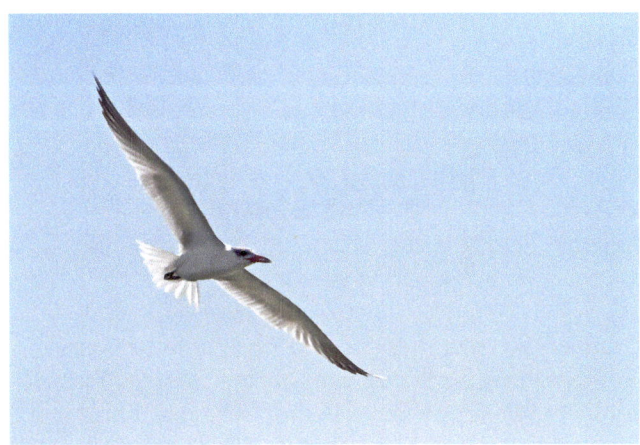

Caspian tern showing the extent of its wingspan. Omokoroa, Tauranga. September.

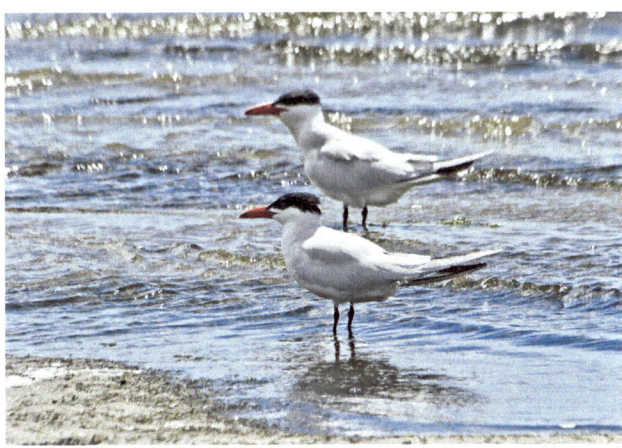

Caspian terns in breeding plumage showing a slight crest. Matua foreshore, Tauranga Harbour. November.

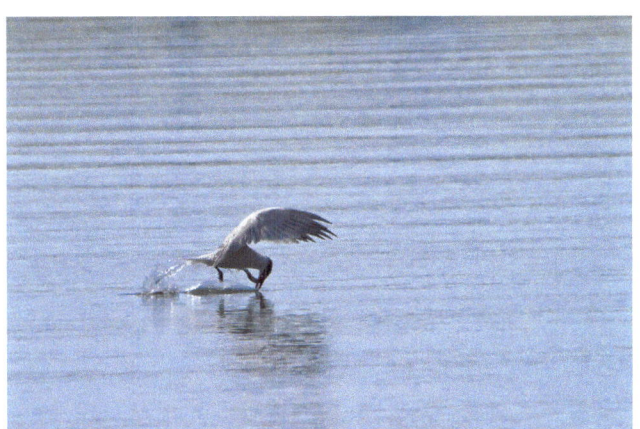

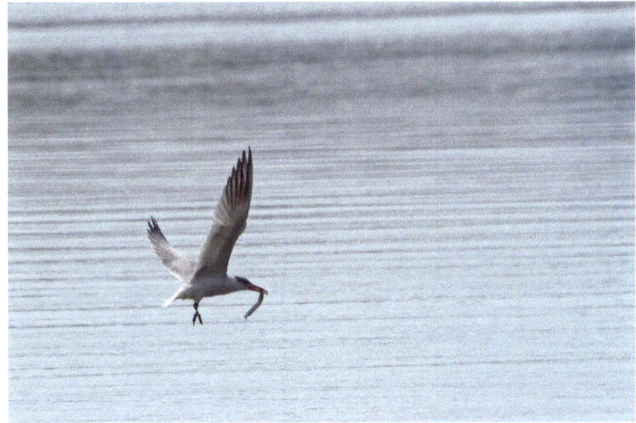

Above and right – Caspian tern fishing. Omokoroa, Tauranga. September.

WHITE-FRONTED TERNS

White-fronted terns are medium sized terns and can often be seen in large groups, especially in winter. The most common site for these is the sand spit formed where a river meets the sea where they are most likely to be seen on the seaward side of the spit. They may also be found near cliffs, in harbours near man-made structures or on estuary sand banks at low tide.

These terns are often seen near red-billed gulls which are larger birds. Birds that inhabit beaches used by people become habituated to human presence to some extent. When with gulls the terns seem more comfortable being approached – possibly because the gulls have a greater tolerance for people and remain relaxed for longer. I also found that the black-fronted terns on the edge of the colony of white-fronted terns were relaxed while the whole colony remained relaxed, even though they were several metres closer to me.

If disturbed the whole flock will fly up then land back in the same spot or another close by.

Adult white-fronted terns are very elegant birds with nice clean lines and clear black, white and light grey. Young birds are mottled with less well defined lines.

White-fronted terns are endemic which means they breed only in New Zealand. Some migrate to Australia for the winter, but with rare exceptions return to New Zealand to breed.

Summers are spent nesting, mainly on the east coast. Some of the birds that remain in New Zealand for the winter may migrate to west coast locations. Others stay fairly close to their nest sites. The birds return to the nest site from which they hatched and begin breeding at three years old. They develop permanent pair bonds after the elaborate courtship rituals shown in the following pages.

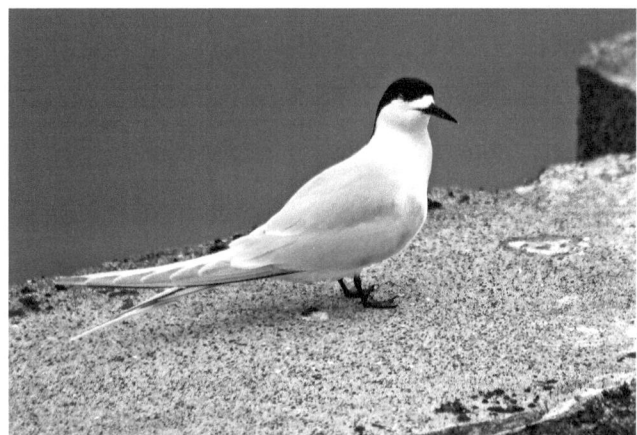

White-fronted tern in breeding plumage and showing a clearly defined black cap and white front. Tauranga Harbour. October.

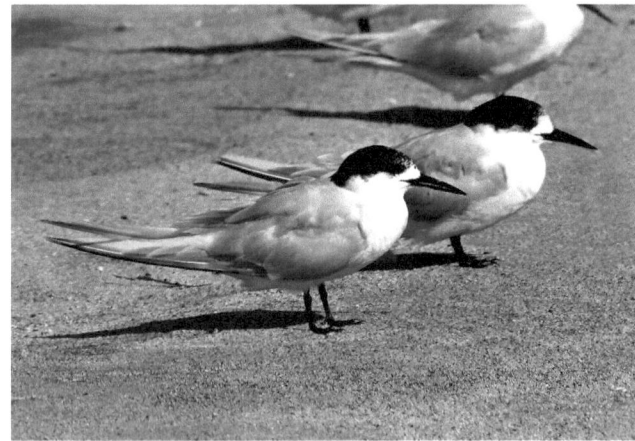

The markings are less well defined when the birds are not in breeding plumage. Ohope, Bay of Plenty. April.

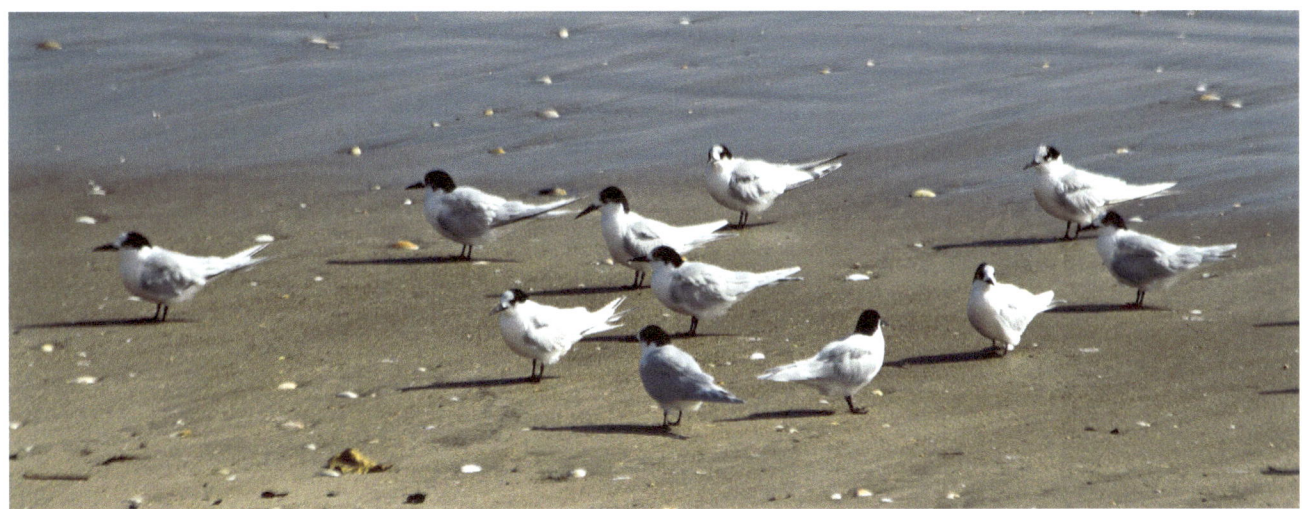
White-fronted terns. Taipa, Northland. April.

Often nesting colonies will have several hundred birds, or the birds may nest alone or in small goups.

The usual nest is just a scrape in sand or rocks, although man made structures appear to be readily used as shown in the sections below. One or two eggs are laid, but normally only one chick survives. The first flight is at about five weeks old.

White-fronted terns mainly feed on small fish and will sometimes join sea birds in a kahawai workup although they don't feed very far out to sea.

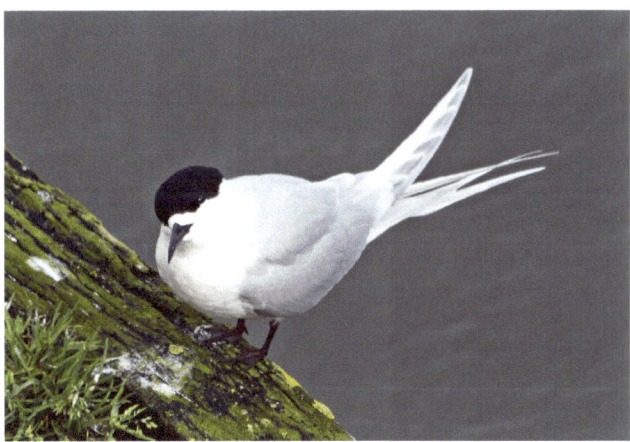
White-fronted tern checking out the camera. Tauranga Harbour. October.

Their life span is about twenty years and there are possibly up to 20,000 pairs in New Zealand. They are not endangered as a species, but are indvidually vulnerable to the habitat destruction also affecting so many other birds.

COURTSHIP

There is little distinction between male and female terns except perhaps size – males may be a little larger. The breeding plumage shows bright, clean, colours with clear delineation between the black, white and grey. In white-fronted terns the chest may be very slightly cream or even pink toned.

When viewing terns, about the only way to tell male from female is that when they are preparing to breed, the male is the one carrying fish to show off to the females. He appears to be demonstrating that he is a good provider.

During the courtship rituals, the appearance of a male with a fish may cause a disturbance throughout the resting colony – especially if two males carrying fish arrive at the same time. The colony is likely to fly up as if disturbed, circle around and re-settle close by.

Once formed, pairs stay together long term and return to the same nest site each year.

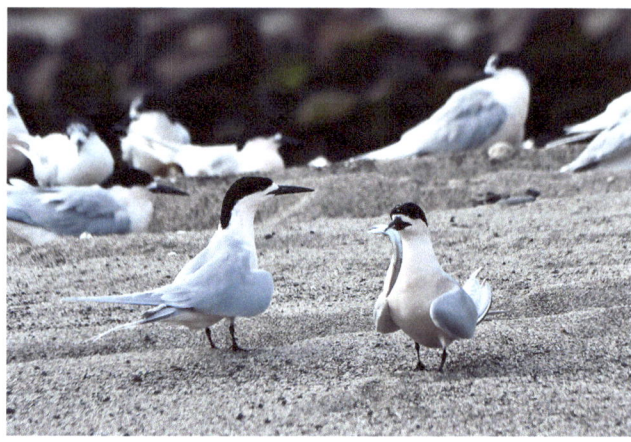

The male white-fronted tern has landed with his 'catch'. **Below left:** *This time no one paid any attention. At other times he seems to be well received and appears to have caught the eye of the female* (Above and below). *Note the colour of the chest above.* These photos Thornton, Bay of Plenty. July.

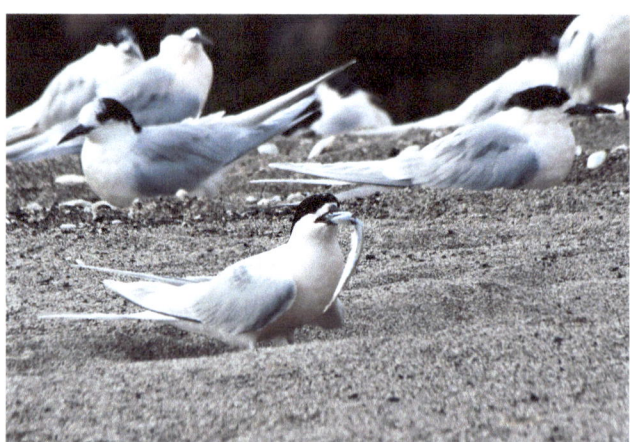

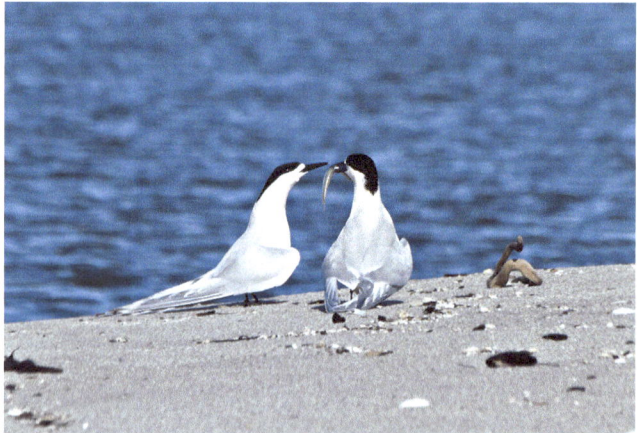

14

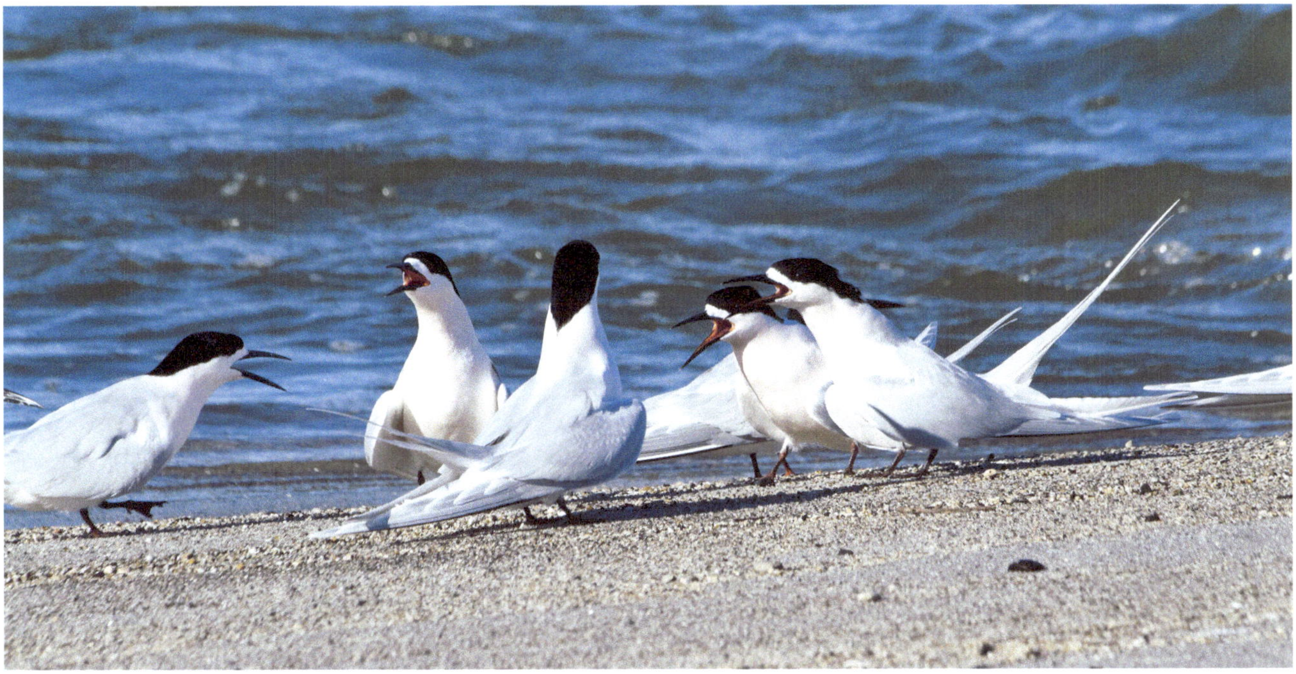

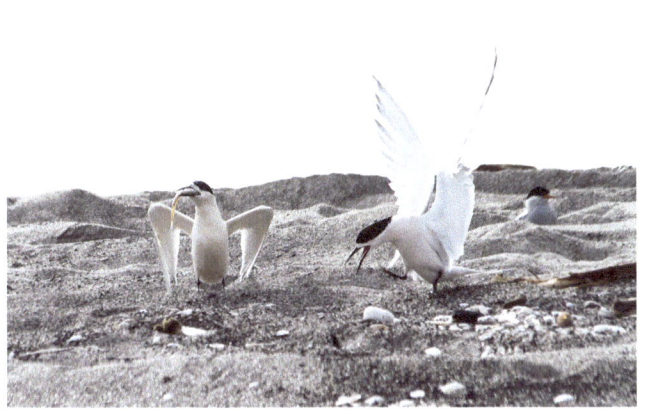

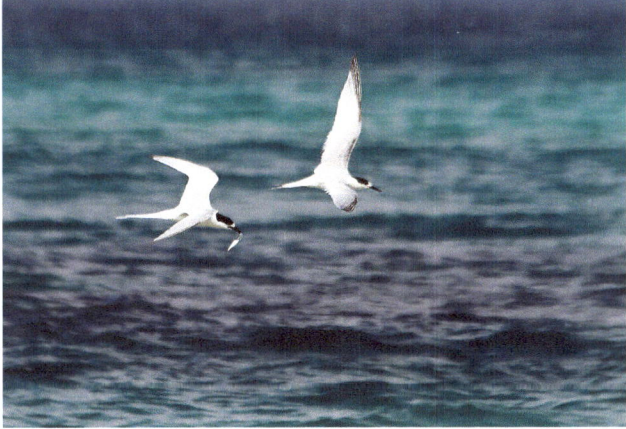

The male carries the fish around for some time, both landing to present it to the females (above and below left), and flying around with them (below right). There may be several females flying with the male at first, but they drop off one by one and the one that is left alone with him becomes his mate. He may then feed the fish to her. Or sometimes he will eat it himself. Thornton, Bay of Plenty, July. Also Kapowairua, Far North. November (below right).

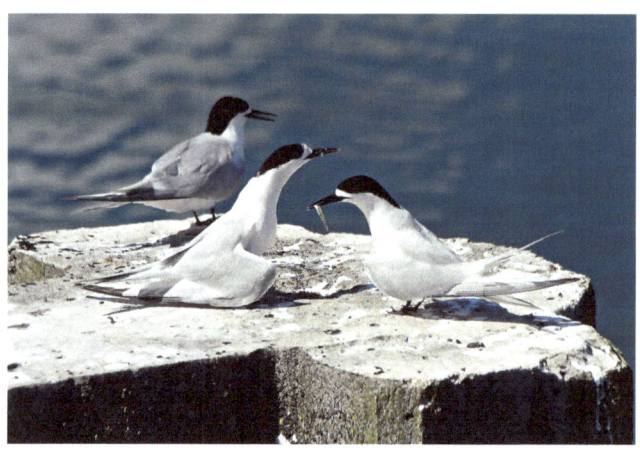 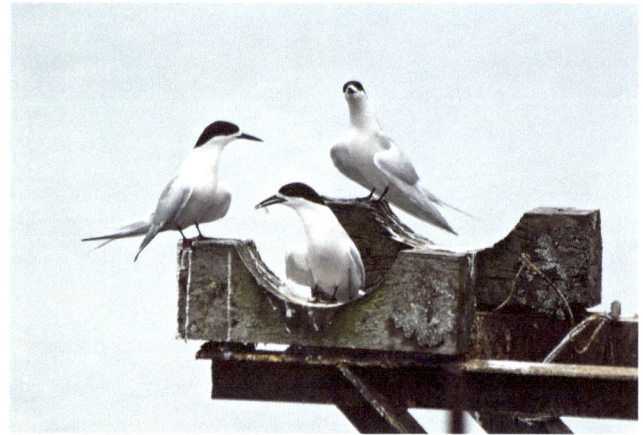

The courtship display also includes the straight necked, lowered wing position seen in these three photos. All Tauranga Harbour. Above left January. Others October.

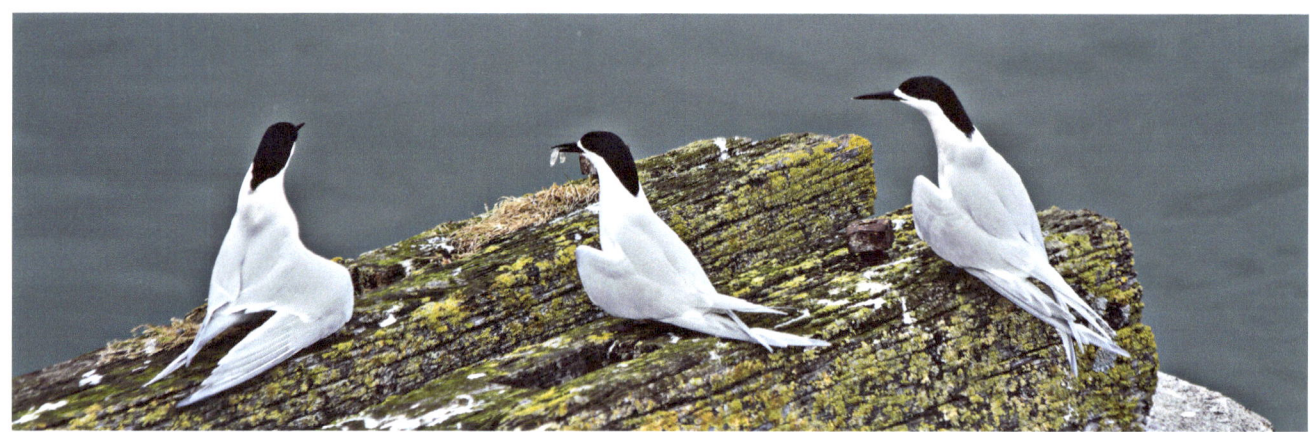

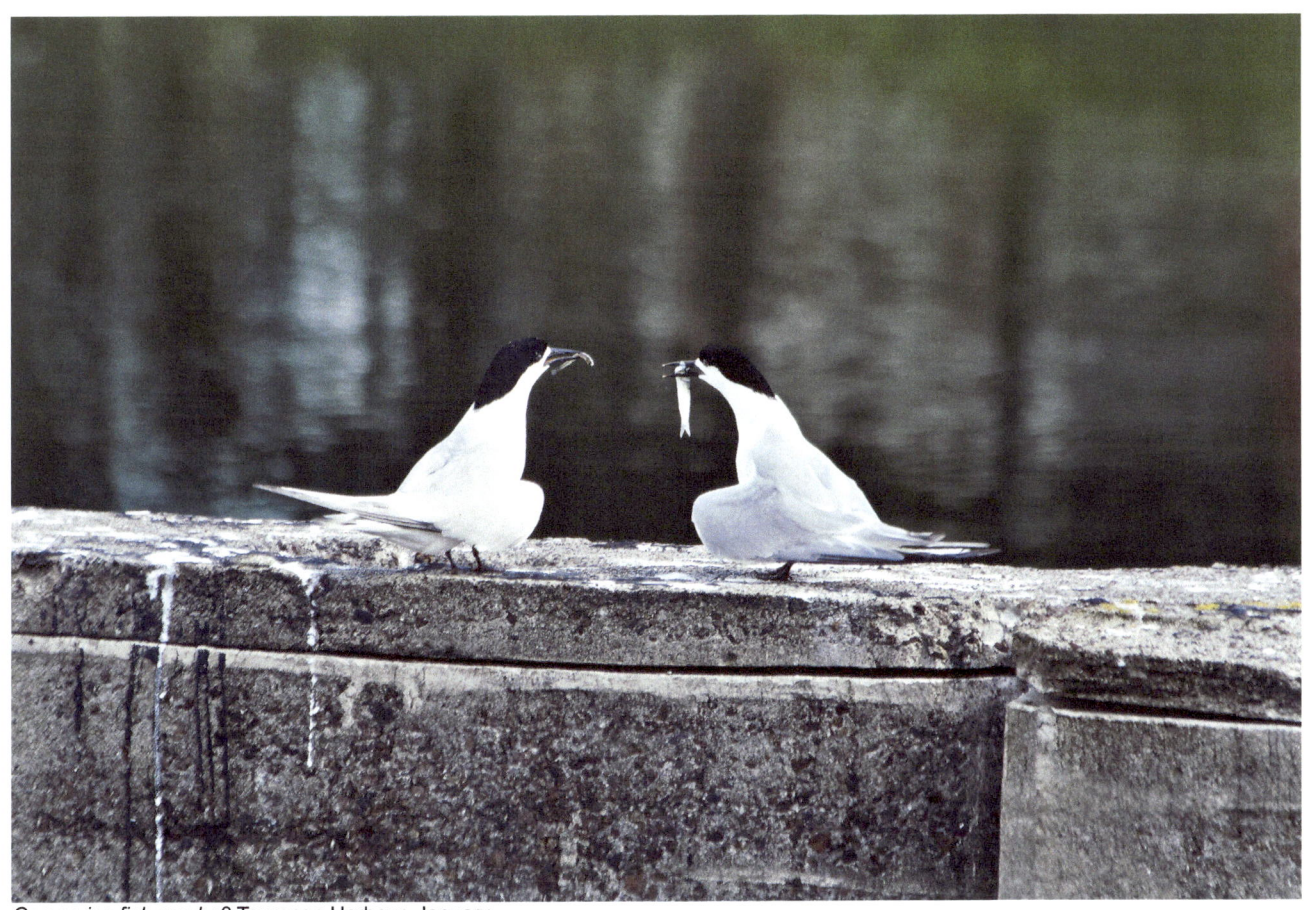

Comparing fish maybe? Tauranga Harbour. January.

NESTING

The photos in this section were taken at a nest site in Tauranga Harbour. The Hairini Bridge is part of a major thoroughfare into the city, with thousands of vehicles passing every day, plus numbers of cyclists and pedestrians. Photographers are also often seen at the site.

The current bridge was built in 1962 and the remains of the old bridge adjacent to it are the home of a colony of white-fronted terns.

In one season 12 pairs of birds raised seven young to fledging. At least two of these were killed by traffic when they started to fly. They had lived with the traffic next to them and with no knowledge of its danger were likely to land in the middle of the road during their early experimental flights.

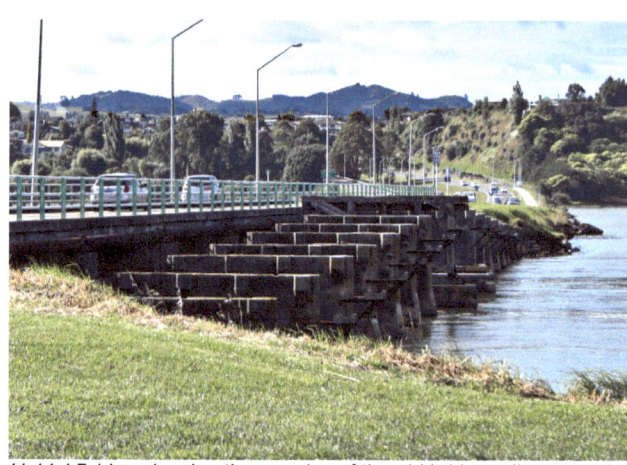

Hairini Bridge showing the remains of the old bridge adjacent to the current bridge. The highest point in the centre has some old timber cross beams still attached to the concrete foundations. The birds mainly nest in hollows in the timber, but the last to stake a claim may be left with just concrete structures. The bridge guard rail has been replaced since the photo above was taken. The new one is less photographer friendly. All three photos October.

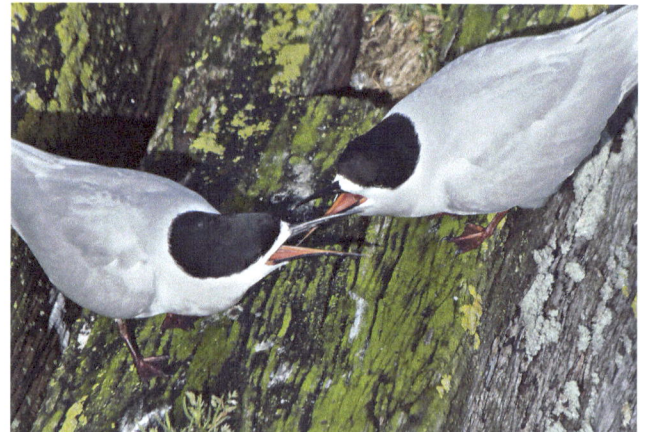

This pair, close to laying, performed this open mouthed communication for several minutes before one flew off.

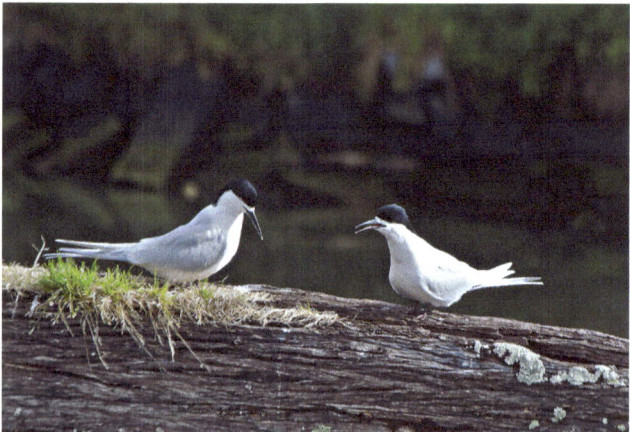

Checking out the nest site.

18

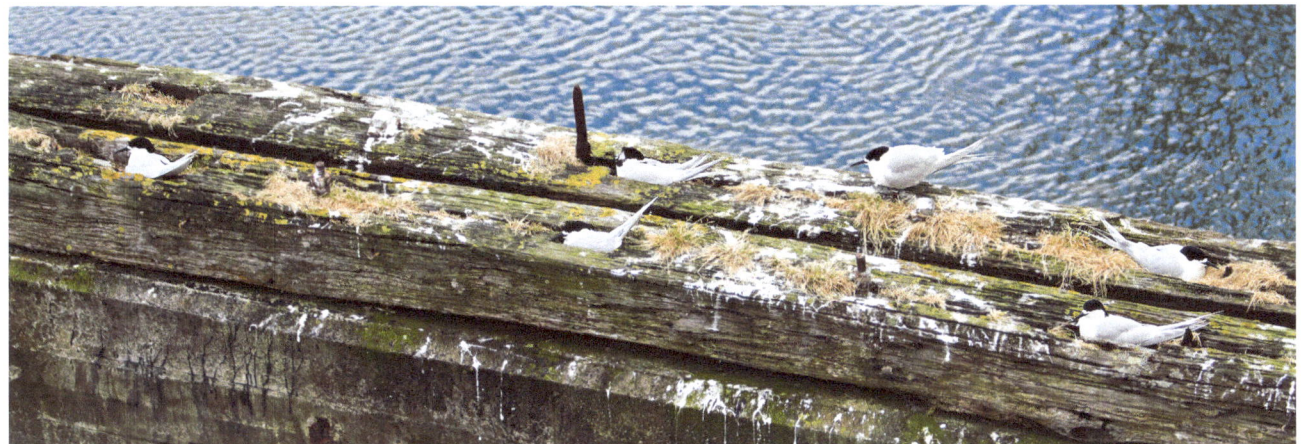

A wide view of part of the nest area. Five birds are sitting on eggs. One empty hollow can be seen in the top left corner. The bird not at a nest appeared to be an odd individual that didn't have a mate. 12 November.

The birds are used to the constant noise and movement of people and traffic, but recognise the difference when people stop to watch them. Early in the season when the chicks were very young they seemed happy enough about my presence. Occasionally the bird closest to me would sound an alarm call, but when others didn't respond the bird would quickly settle.

In sandy or rocky areas, the nests are just a scrape in the ground. At this site, there are hollows in the old timber beams that the birds just manage to fit into. The hollows start out with grass in them – growing from the previous year's fertiliser. This soon deteriorates once the birds move back.

The nests I could see into had one egg each and in most of the others one chick per nest hatched. Any that started with two chicks soon had only one, which I believe is normal for terns – the stronger of the two survives at the expense of its sibling.

I missed the hatching, but the chicks all seemed to be about the same age, except for one late one that was probably from a second clutch.

Both parents shared the care of their eggs. They alternated feeding and nesting sessions, and also spent time together on the nest. The colony looked quite crowded at times with the nests as close together as they were.

There was a lot of communication among the birds, both vocal and non-vocal. A bird sitting on a nest would sometimes lean aggressively towards its neighbour, especially when the neighbour's mate arrived.

Sitting birds greeted their mates vocally when they flew in and there seemed to be a recognition ritual. It was as if they were checking that responsibility was being handed over to the right bird.

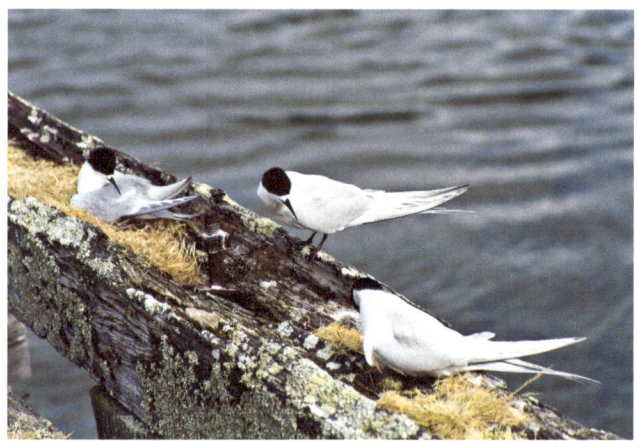

Some of the nests were very close together. 12 November.

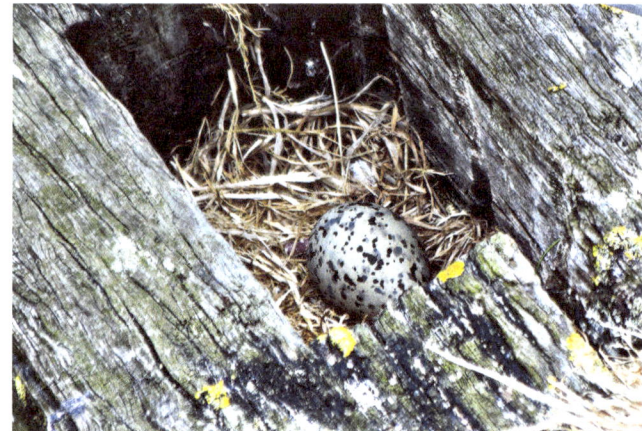

The eggs laid in these hollows were safe from falling out. 19 November.

The photos with precise dates are all from the same season to show the timing of various stages of nesting and developement of the young. Undated photos are from the stated month, but from a different season.

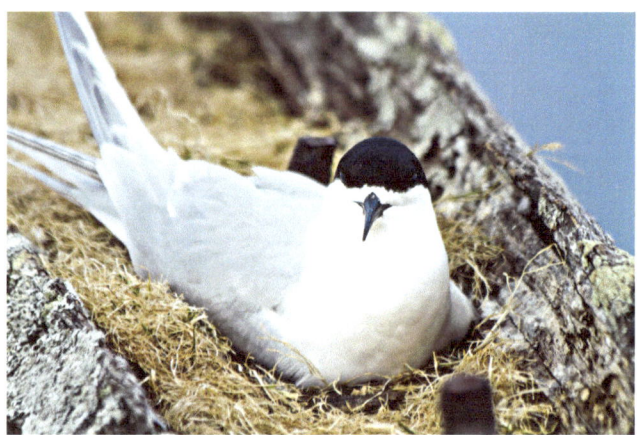

Some nest spaces were the right size. 12 November.

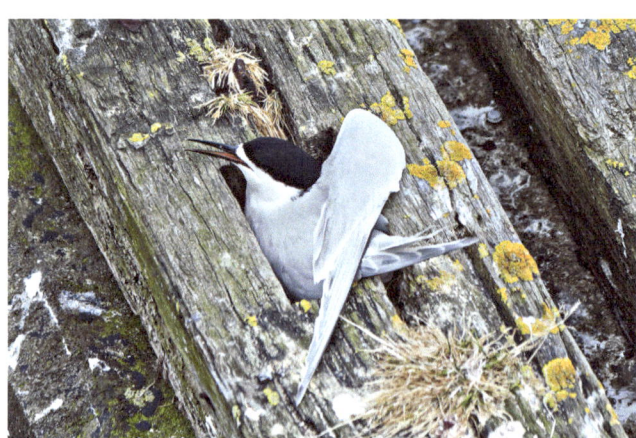

Some spaces were a very tight fit. 19 November.

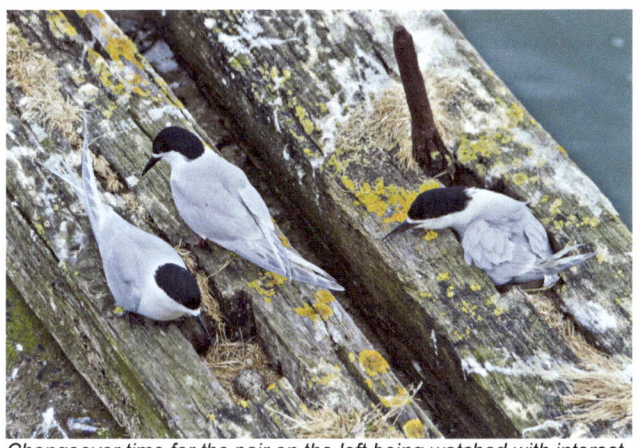

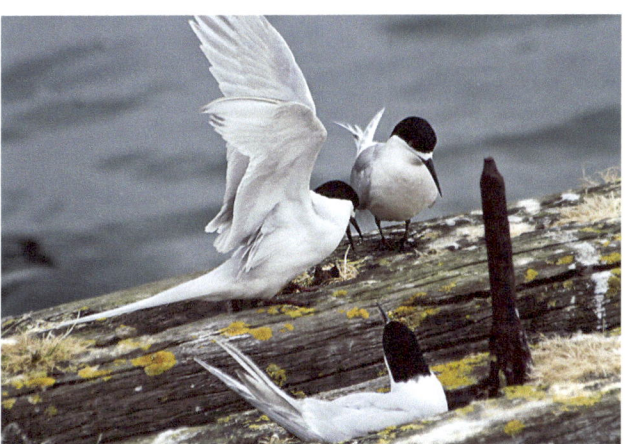

Changeover time for the pair on the left being watched with interest by the neighbour. Above and Above right. 19 November.

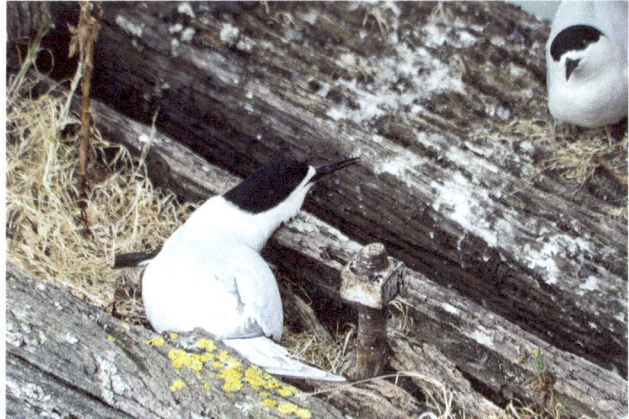

This bird seemed to be trying to attract attention from its mate. 19 November.

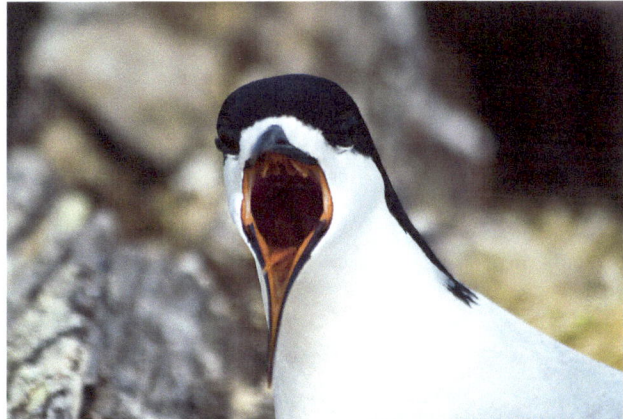

At first I thought this was a message for me, then realised the bird was greeting its mate who was flying in over my head. 12 November.

Sometimes one member of a pair sat near but slightly apart from the nest. Its mate on the nest would lean towards the other bird as if it were trying to communicate but was ignored.

Overall, the contstant calling and movement made the colony a very busy and noisy place.

Of the three species of tern in this book, the Caspian tern has the shortest incubation period at approximately 21 days. The black-fronted tern is a few days longer at up to 24 days. The white fronted tern incubates its eggs for up to 27 days.

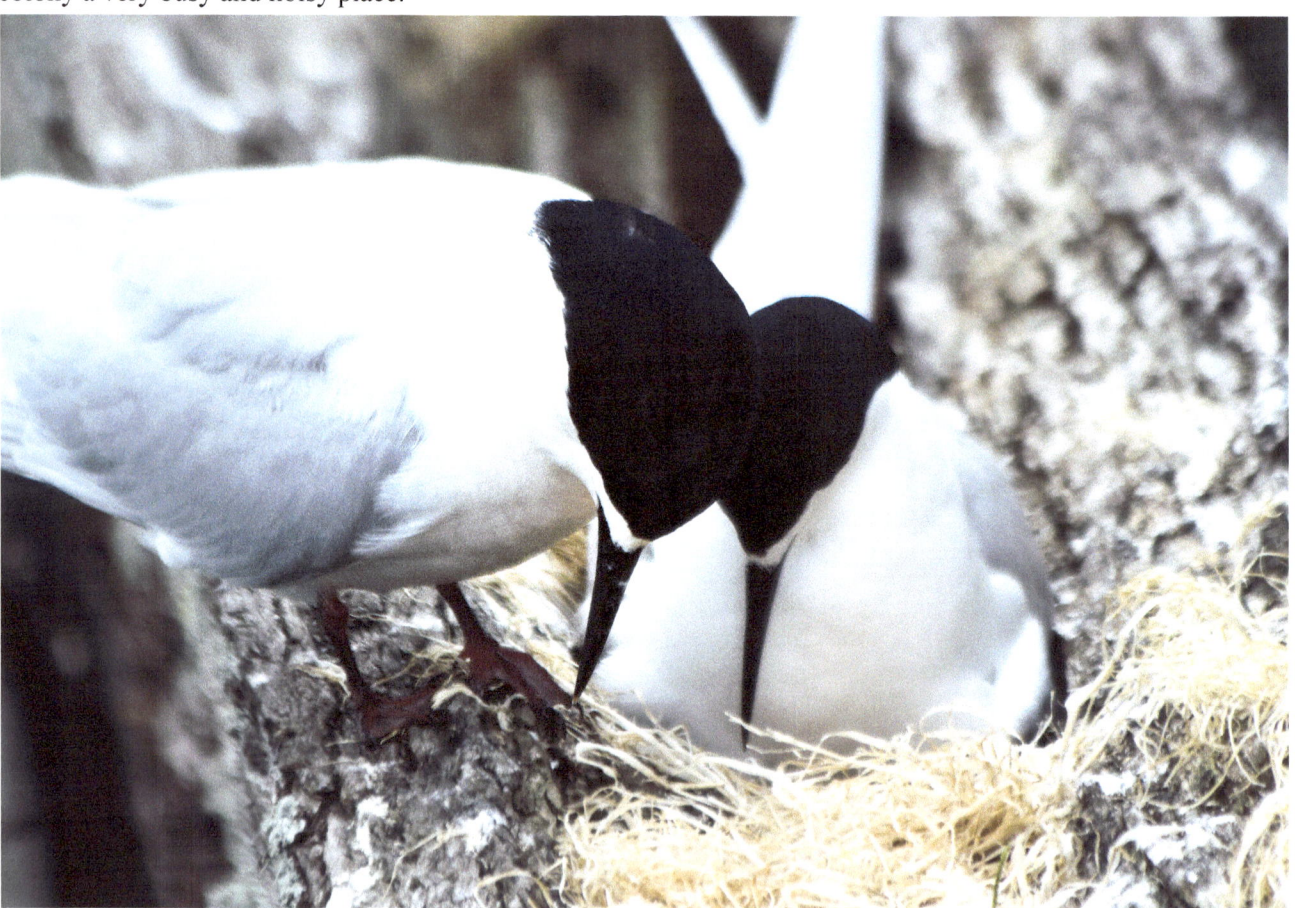

Together at the nest. 19 November.

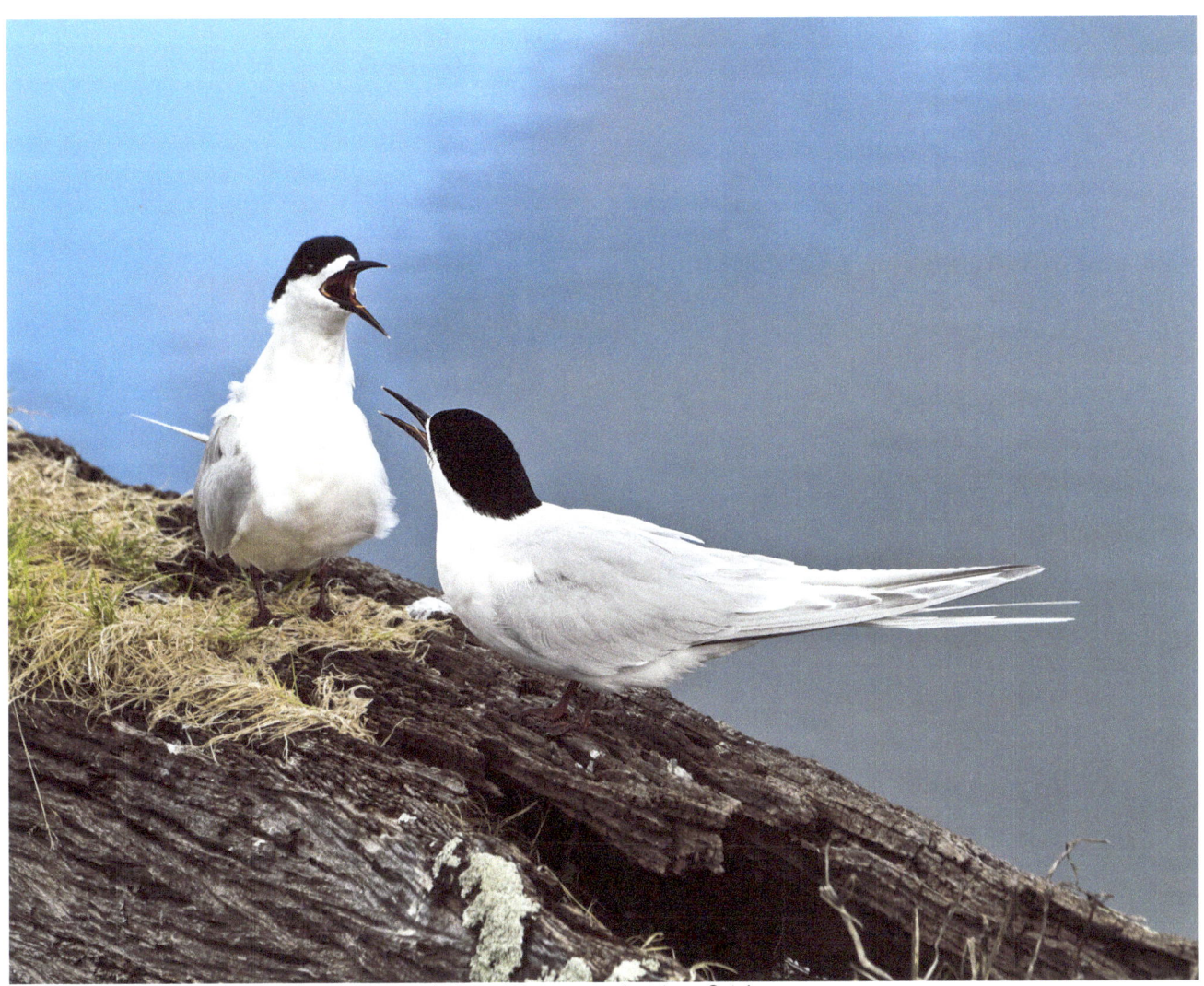
The vocal nature of the terns' communication made the colony a very noisy place. October.

RAISING THE FAMILY

When the eggs hatched the hard work started for the parents. For the next several weeks their whole existence was focused on feeding and protecting their young. The colony became busier and noisier than ever with the constant movement of birds bringing food.

At first the birds seemed quite relaxed about my presence, but as the chicks grew, the parents became more wary. This was apparent from increased alarm calls and although they stayed on the nests, they clearly weren't totally happy and I backed off a bit. This late insecurity is possibly an awareness of their vulnerability to attack by aerial predators.

The chicks mainly stayed within the confines of the nests, but sometimes moved around a little. The attending parent would call to the wandering chick, presumably warning it to come back to the safety of the nest. These forays were only about 30 centimetres or so, so no real distance, but each pair mantained its own space within the limits of the closeness of the nests.

Usually one parent stayed at the nest while the other went fishing. Occasionally a chick would be left totally unattended for a short time.

This nest site was possibly more contained and provided a safer location than precarious cliff tops might have been, but it still had its risks. There were gaps between the lengths of timber that some chicks fell through to the ledge below. If the weather was warm and dry and the parents able to reach them to feed, these chicks survived. Unfortunately at least two did not.

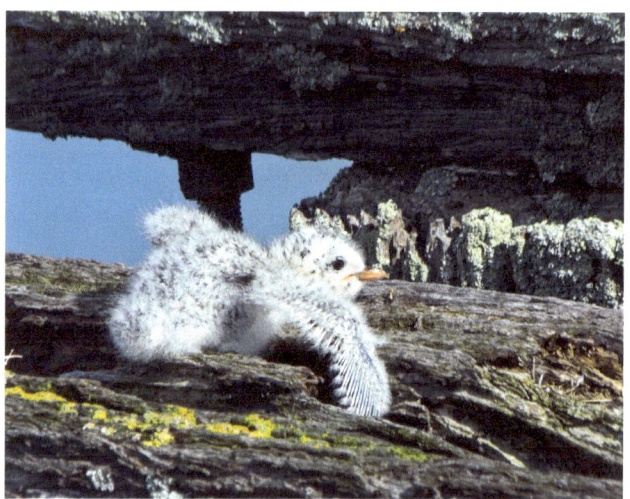

A newly hatched chick moving within the nest site. 4 December.

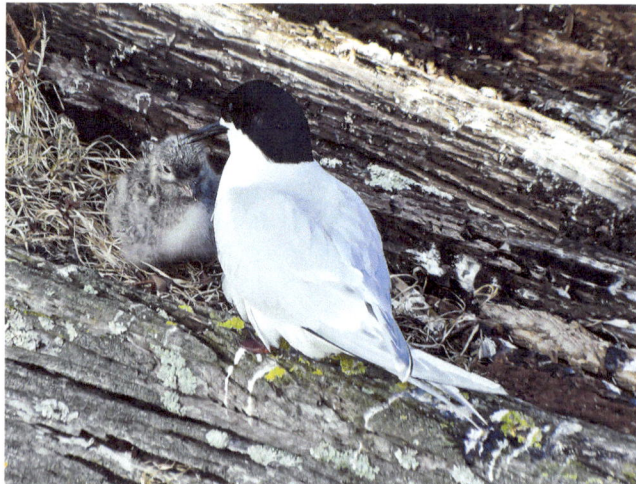

A different chick - already fluffy and cute. 4 December.

The food was fed directly to the chicks with the only requirement being that it was small enough to fit into the recipient's mouth. Some of the fish brought did look too big, but the chicks grabbed it eagerly and it was amazing to see just how large a fish they could cope with.

The chicks all fed very hungrily, with one exception. One chick seemed almost reluctant to take food. It had hatched later than the others and was slower growing. The parents seemed a bit bewildered that it didn't grab the food hungrily, but they perservered with trying to feed it and, surprisingly, it did survive.

When the birds on the nests weren't actively feeding, they rested. The chicks quickly grew too big to sleep under the parent, but would snuggle up closely. The parent would rest with its head tucked into its back, but usually with its eyes open and watching me.

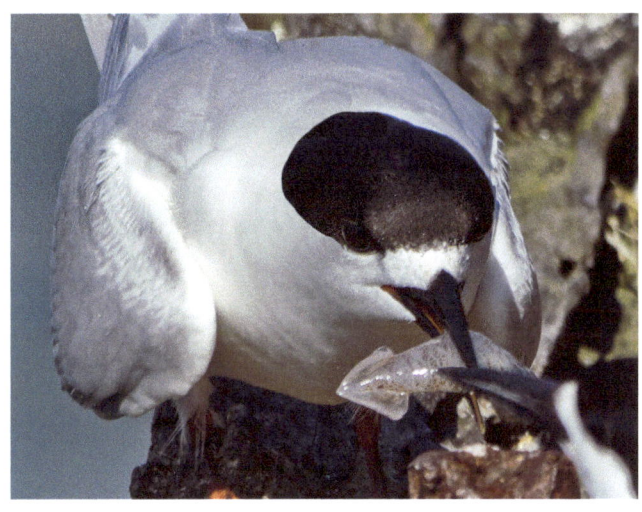

Food was the primary focus for the chicks and was brought frequently throughout the day. There was variety in the diet as shown in the three photos here – clockwise from above is a baby squid, a shrimp and the small fish that make up the majority of the diet. (Photos 4, 6 and 17 Devember).

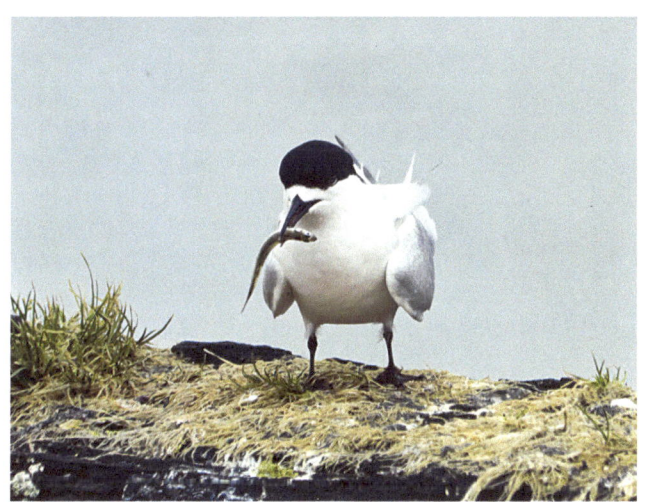

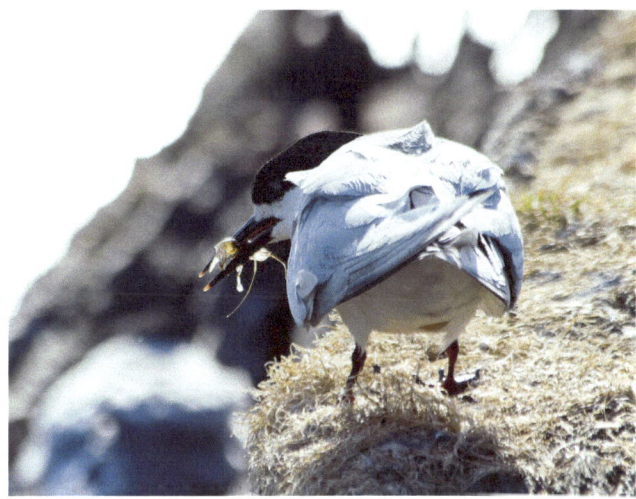

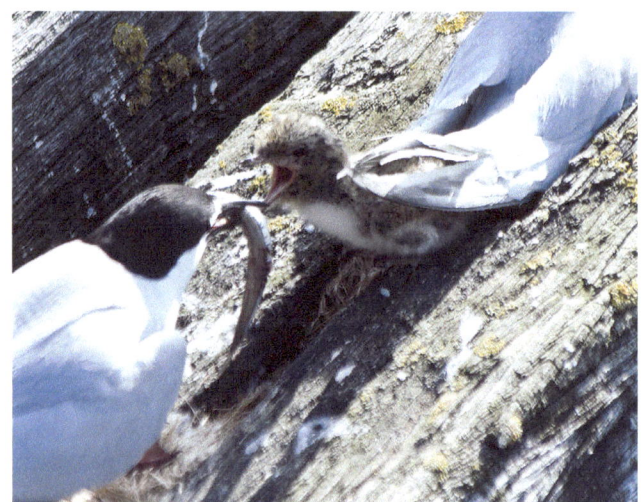

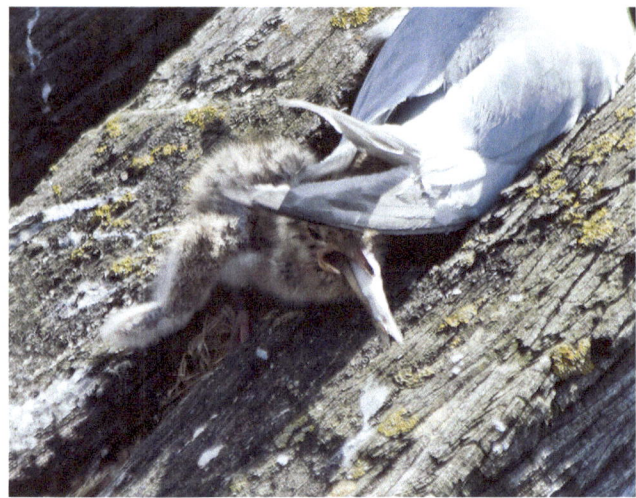

Above and below - the fish looks far too big to fit...

...but with a bit of manipulation it went down. 6 December.

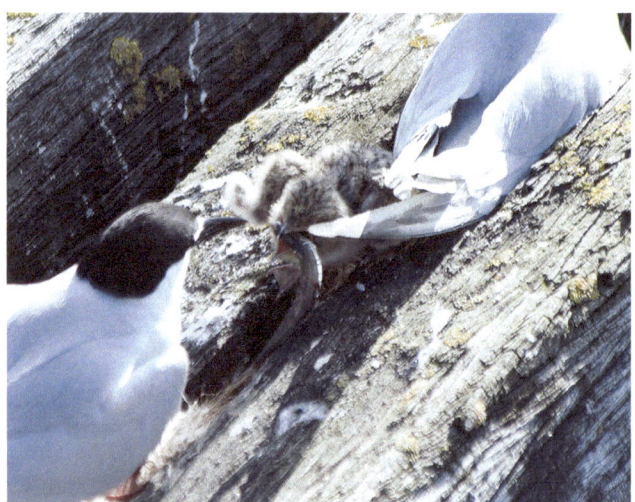

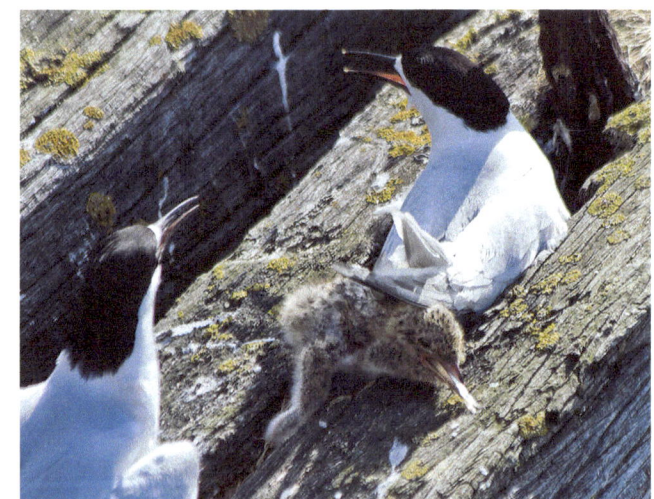

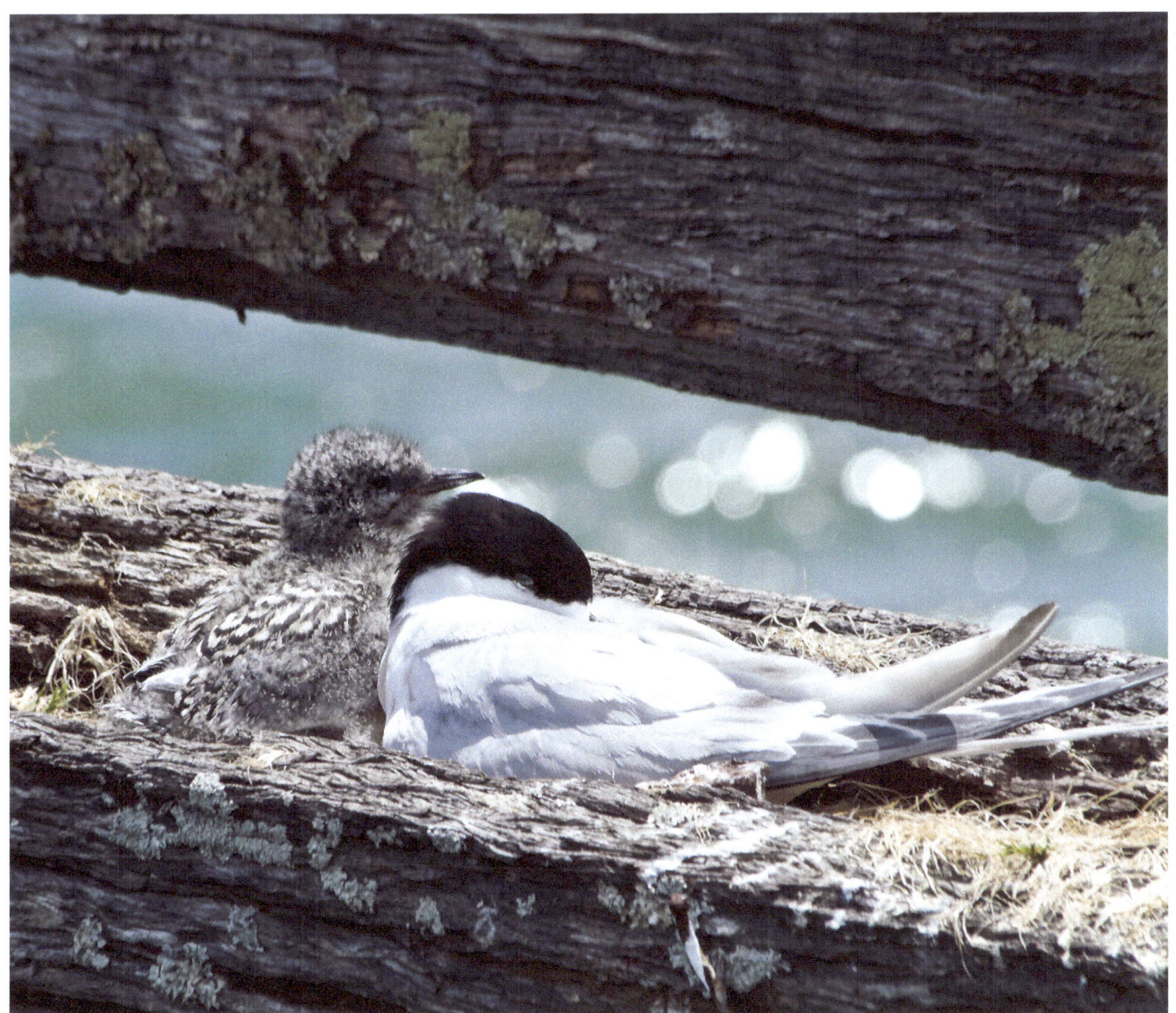

A quiet momont of rest, but still with an eye on the camera. 10 December.

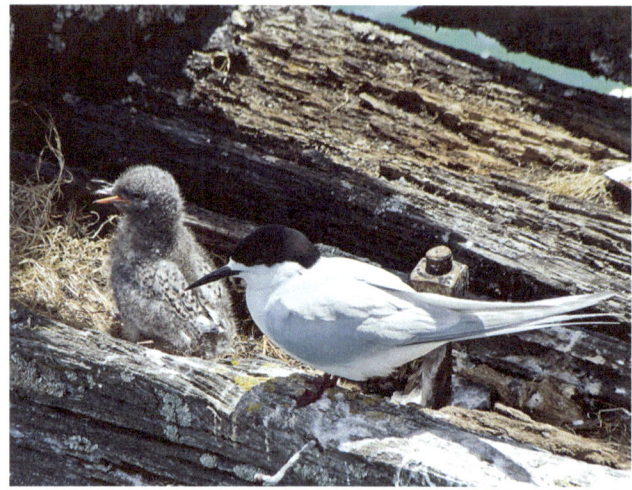

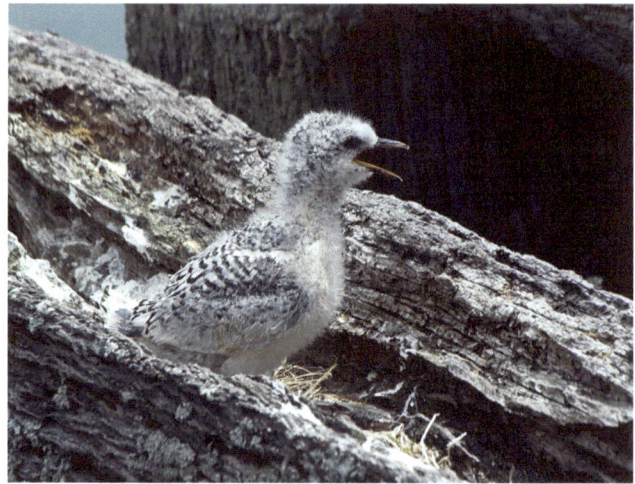

Alert and looking for the next feed (above). It arrived about a minute later (below). 10 December.

Home alone. 13 December.

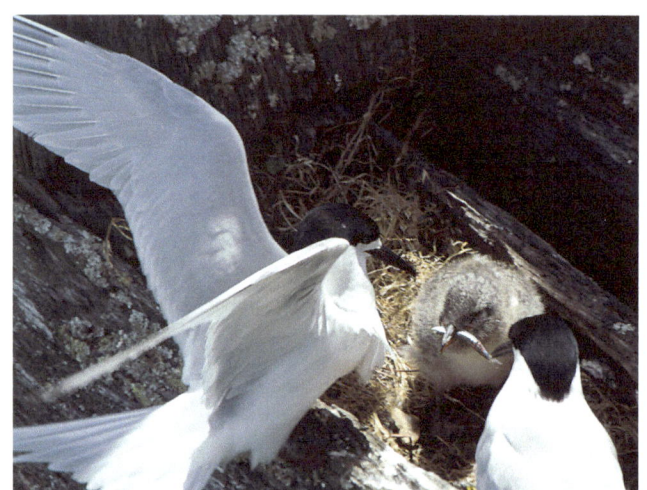

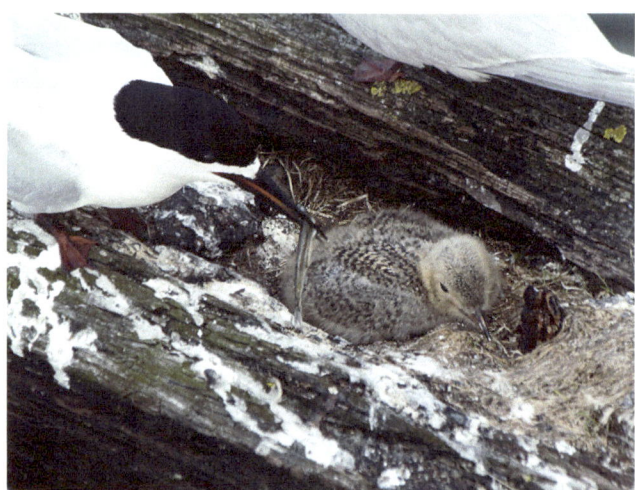

This late hatchling was a reluctant feeder. 24 December.

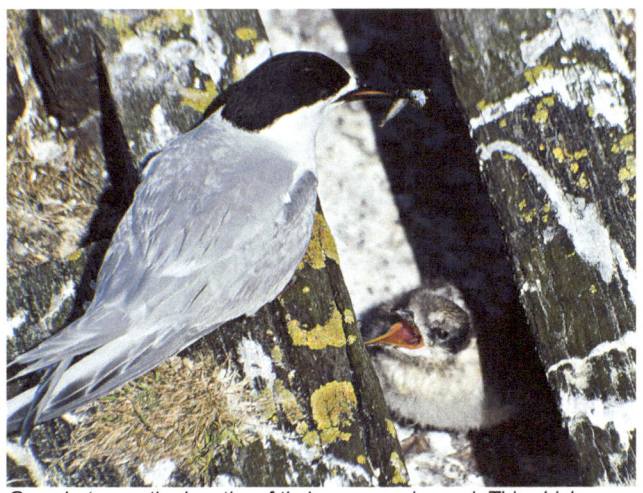

Gaps between the lengths of timber were a hazard. This chick was lucky – the weather was warm and dry and the parent able to feed it. 3 January.

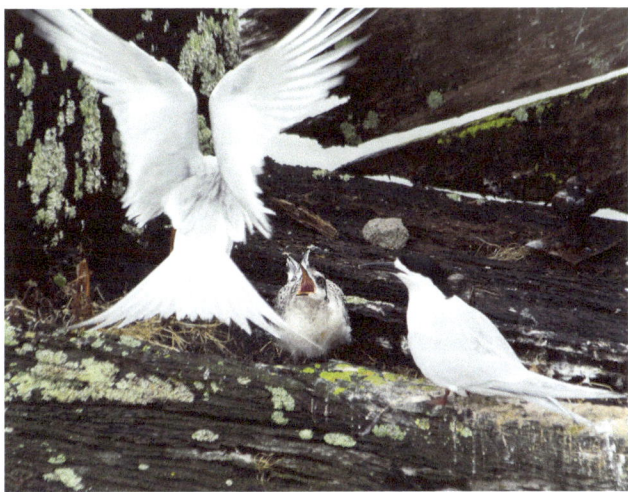

Another feed arriving. 17 December.

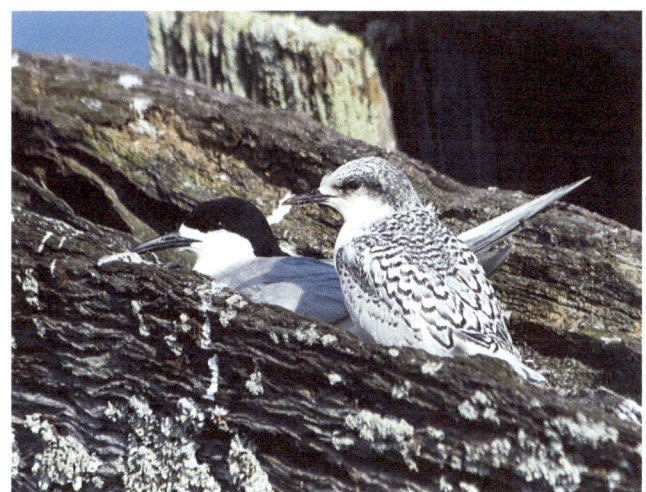

As the feathers grew the juvenile colour patterns emerged. 24 December.

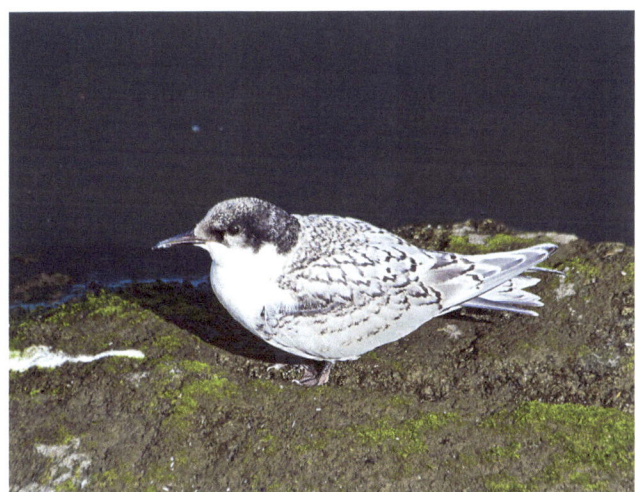

By Christmas some babies started to venture out of the nest. 24 December.

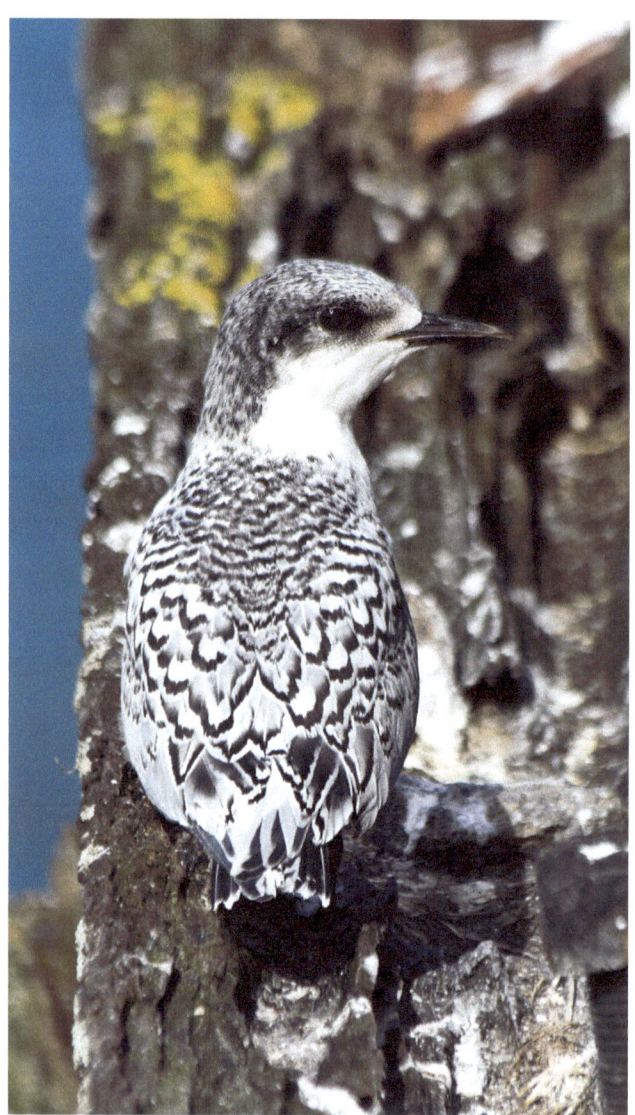

By late December the young birds were starting to look quite grown-up. 24 December.

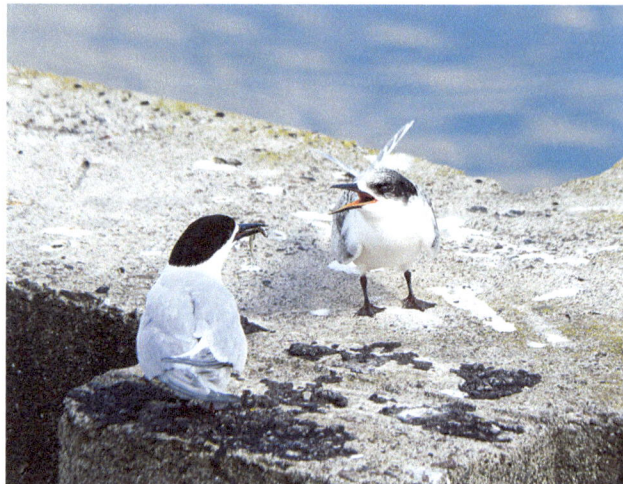

Being fed was still top priority. Above 3 January. Below 14 January.

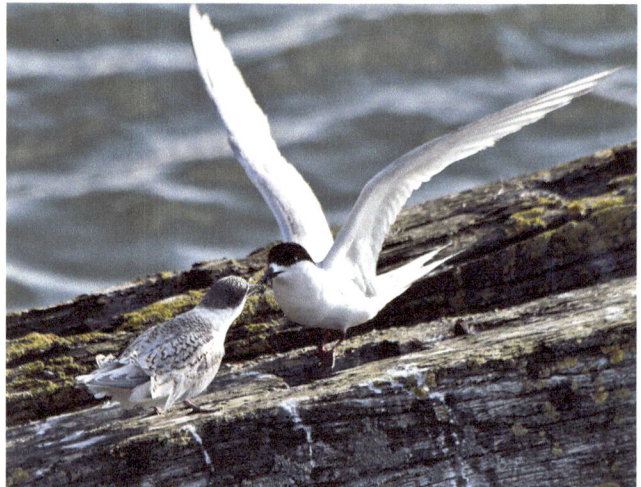

White-fronted terns have also nested on the top of an old wharf pile in the harbour right next to Tauranga's CBD. Near the nest site is a popular local restaurant that offers a great view of the birds' activity.

This was a single pair with two babies, of which only one survived. The adult birds were very wary of people walking past and when I stopped to watch them I was buzzed. The bird flew over my head aggressively, not quite touching me, and it was very clear that I was an unwelcome intruder.

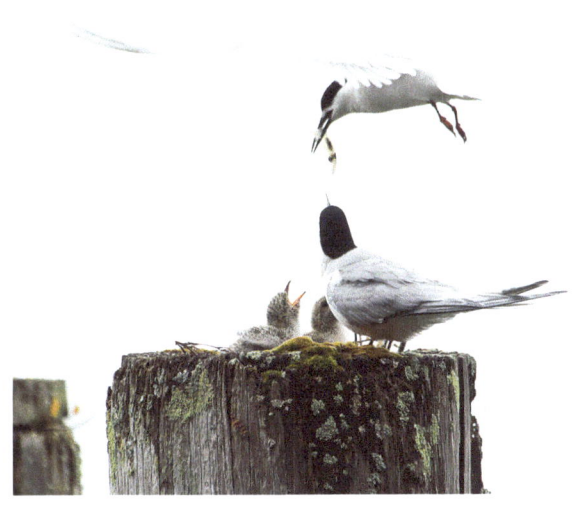

Fortunately the board walkway was sheltered by pohutukawa trees and there was a spot where I could watch the nest unobserved. The photos on this page and overleaf are from this nest. All December.

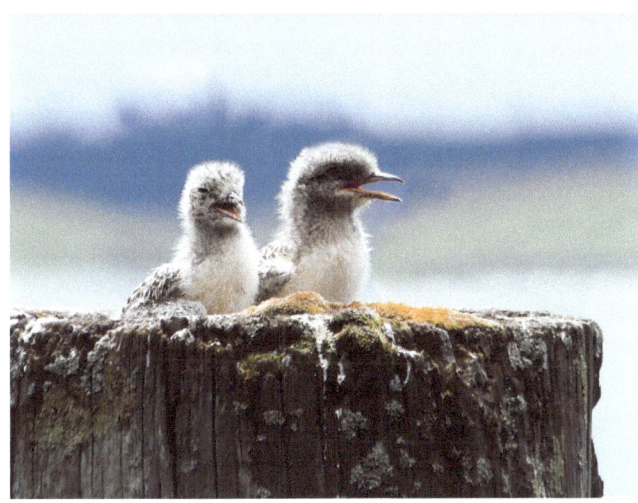

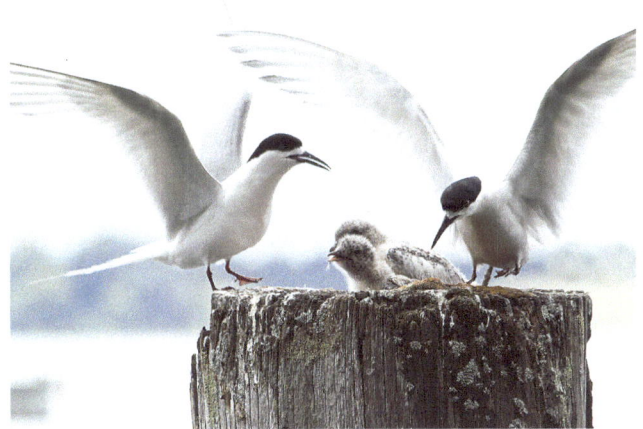

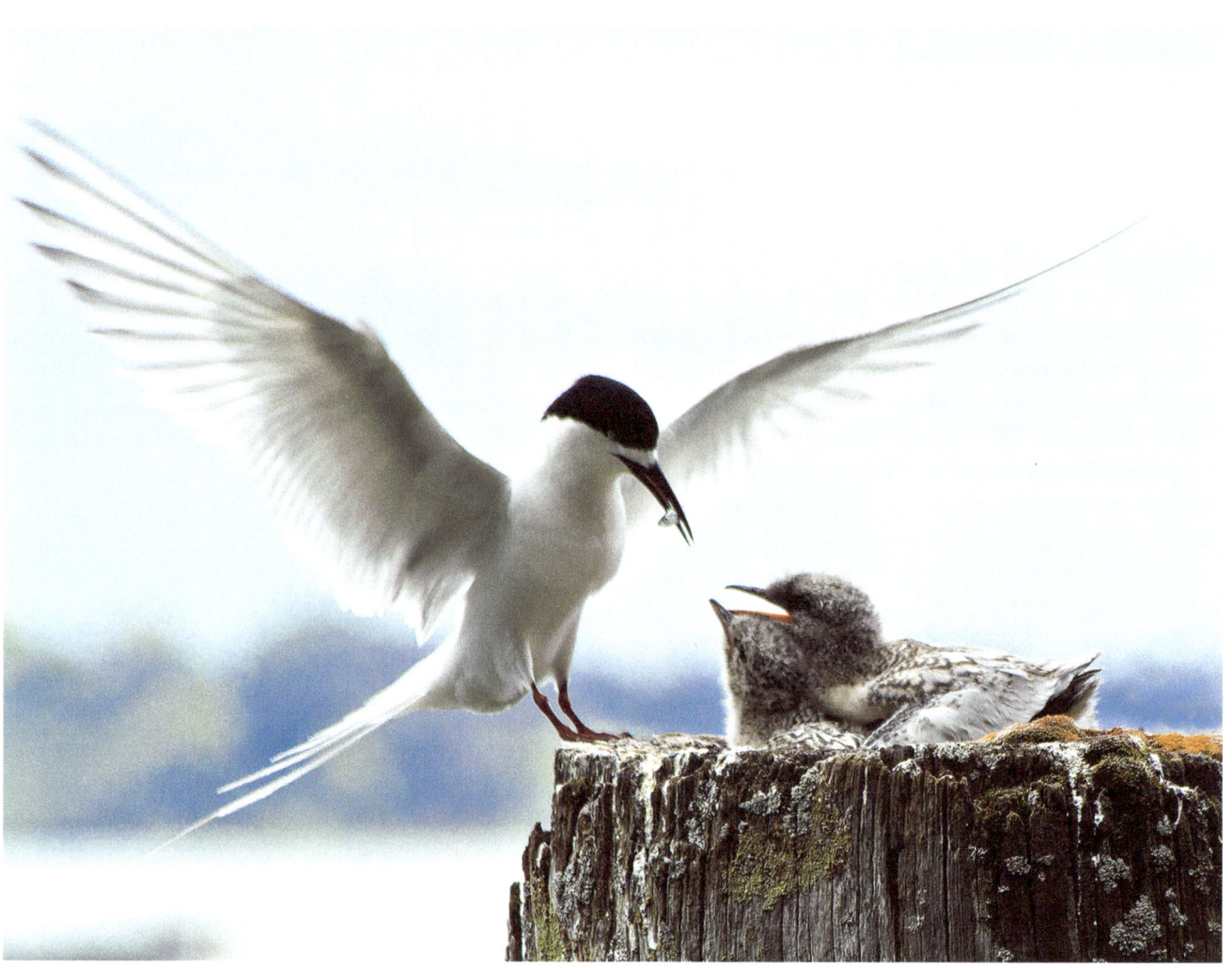

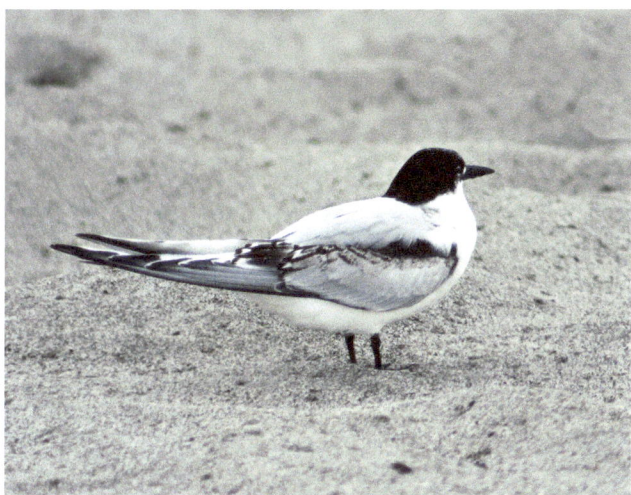

After leaving the nest site the immature white-fronted terns slowly acquire adult colouration. The patterns are variable and can be quite attrractive (Above).

Below, the adult is trying to rest while the young bird continues to demand food. They continue begging in this way for several weeks after fledging. Both photos Thornton, Bay of Plenty. April.

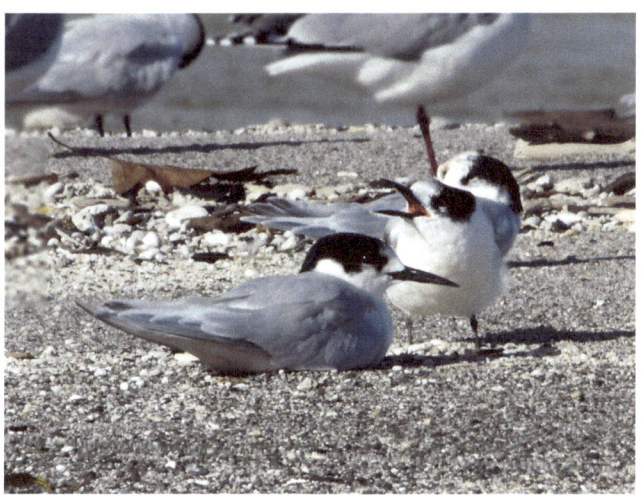

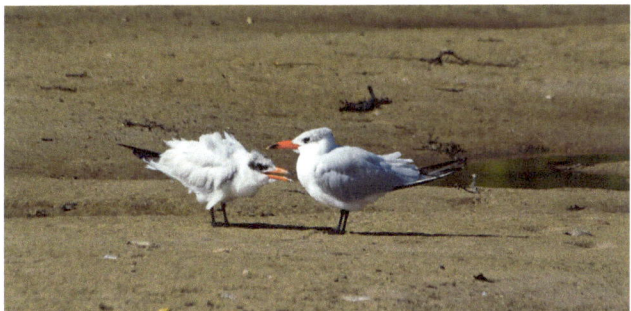

Adult and juvenile Caspian terns. Adults usually stand facing into the wind. The immature bird begging for food faces the opposite way and has its feathers blown about. Its whining is more incessant and ongoing than that of the white-fronted terns. Tauranga Bay, Northland. April.

After the breeding season is over, the young and adult white-fronted terns form flocks. Some migrate to Australia for the winter. Others stay closer to home and can be seen in colonies at many beaches around New Zealand.

Caspian terns form smaller groups and tend to stay closer to their nest sites, often within 100kms.

Black-fronted terns disperse to coastal locations.

In both white-fronted and Caspian terns, juvenile plumage is replaced by adult colours in stages so the immature birds can be clearly identified by this intermediate colouration.

The previous season's young can also be identified by behaviour – they continue begging for food from the adults for quite some time. This can be seen by the typical subordinate stance and heard in the incessant whining sound that can be so annoying.

BATHING AND PREENING

Feathers are very important for birds. They keep the bird warm and dry, allow it to fly, and are also used for communication. It is therefore not surprising that birds spend a lot of time caring for their feathers by bathing and preening.

Bathing is done to clean the feathers. White-fronted and Caspian terns may be seen bathing in either sea water or in the fresh or brackish water of a creek flowing through an estuary at low tide. Bathing is often communal and there may even be other species such as red-billed gulls bathing along with the terns.

Preening is the bird's way of grooming itself. It checks through all its thousands of feathers; straightening, placing and oiling them. The oil comes from special glands near the tail and the bird uses its bill to distribute the oil along the length of each feather.

During the moult feathers may be shed during preening. The old feathers are replaced by new ones growing through from underneath. These keep the bird fresh and healthy, and are how the birds change colour as they mature and signal readiness for pairing by adopting their breeding plumage.

Watching birds preen is interesting because it allows us an opportunity to see their feathers better and to appreciate the colour and structure of them. After a preening session the bird will often stretch and provide a good view of its wings.

Preening may be seen at any time the bird is relaxed and if done in our presence, it indicates that it is fairly happy about us being there, which is always nice.

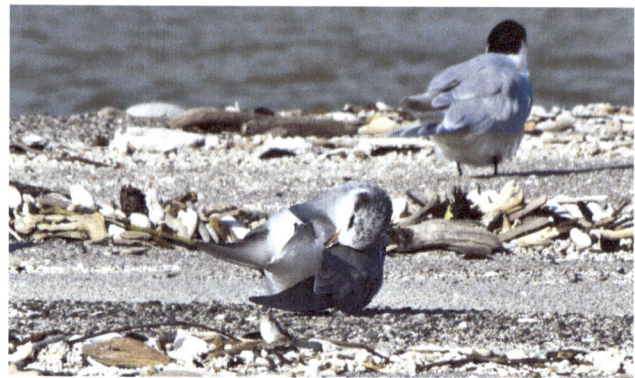

Juvenile black-fronted tern preening. Thornton, Bay of Plenty. April.

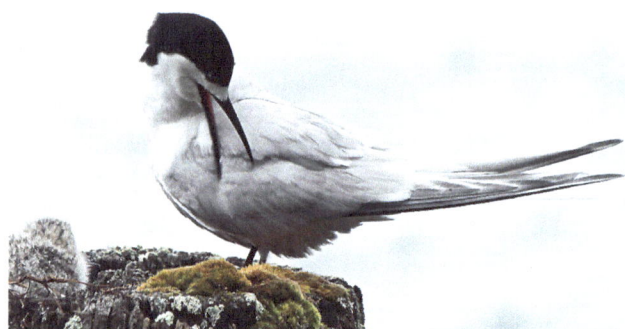

White-fronted tern preening. Above and below Tauranga Harbour. December.

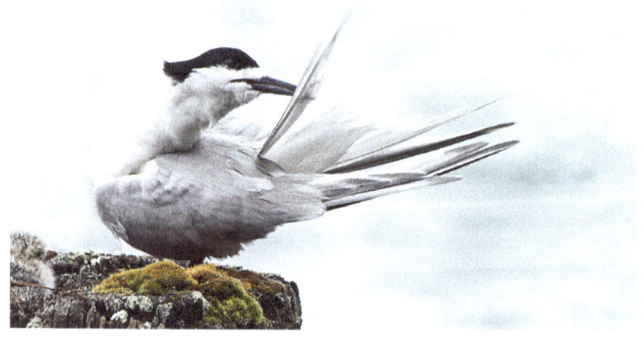

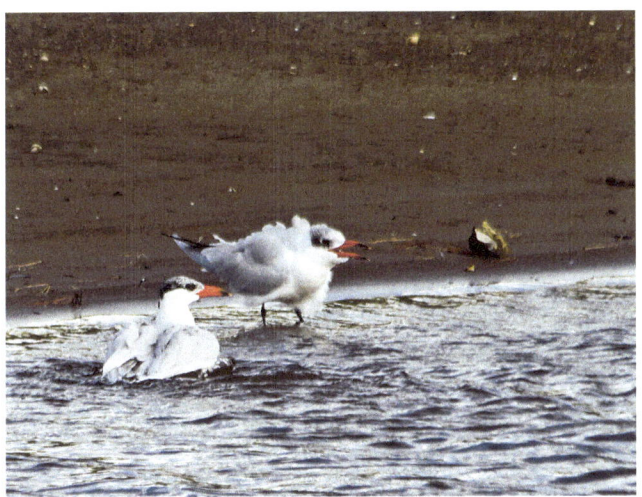

Adult Caspian tern bathing while the immature bird with it just wants to be fed - as always. Tauranga Bay, Northland. April.

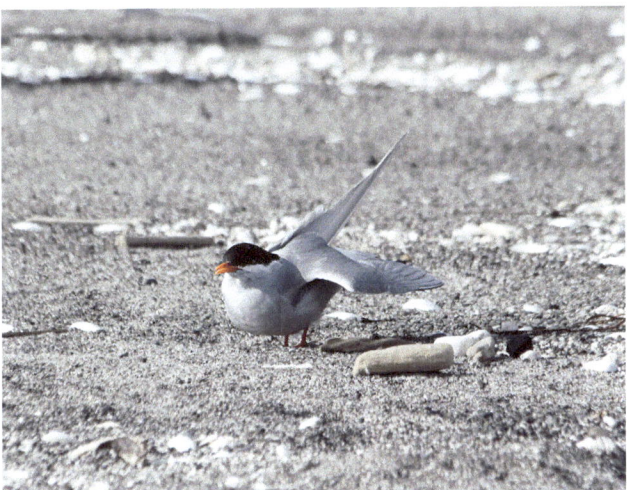

Black-fronted tern stretching its wing. Thornton, Bay of Plenty. July.

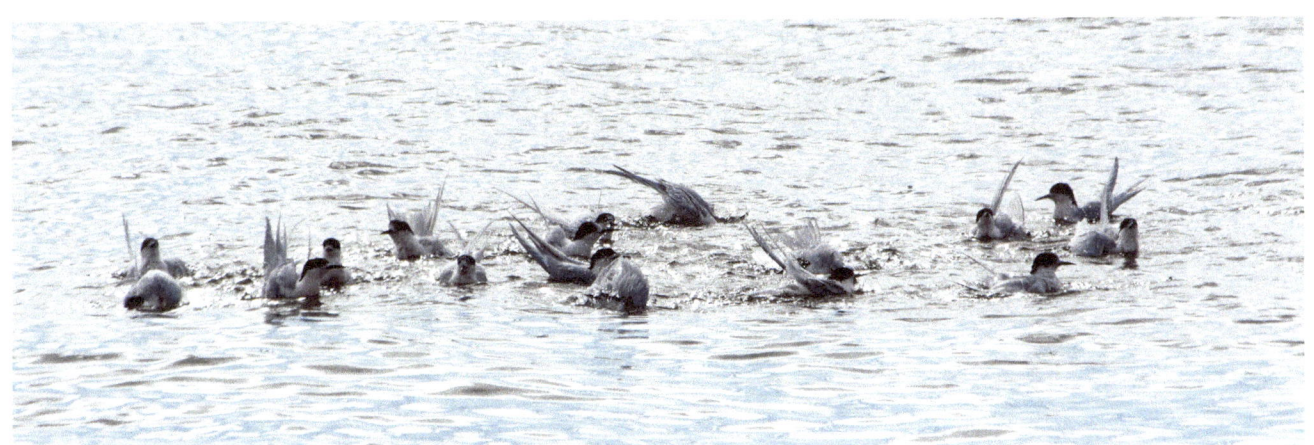

A group of white-fronted terns bathing in the sea. Thornton, Bay of Plenty. July.

TERNS IN FLIGHT

These are a few last photos to show the birds' lives in the air – flying, fishing, courting.

They are always active and are fascinating to watch as they go about their daily lives, working hard to look after themselves and their families.

Whatever they are doing, birds have a great view of the world that we see only from the ground.

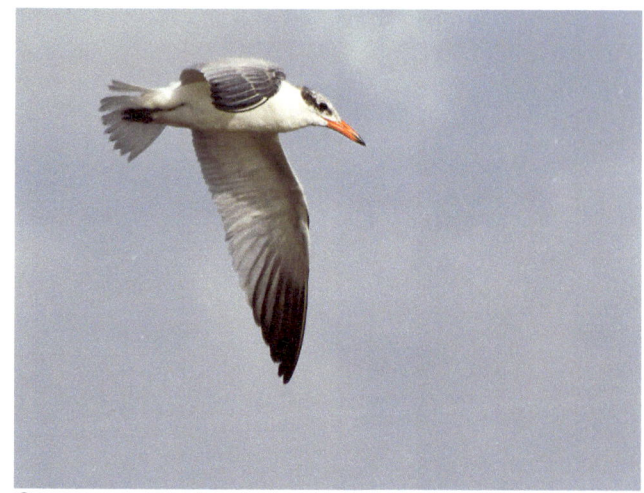

Caspian tern. Note the short and rounded shape of the tail. Tauranga Bay, Northland. April.

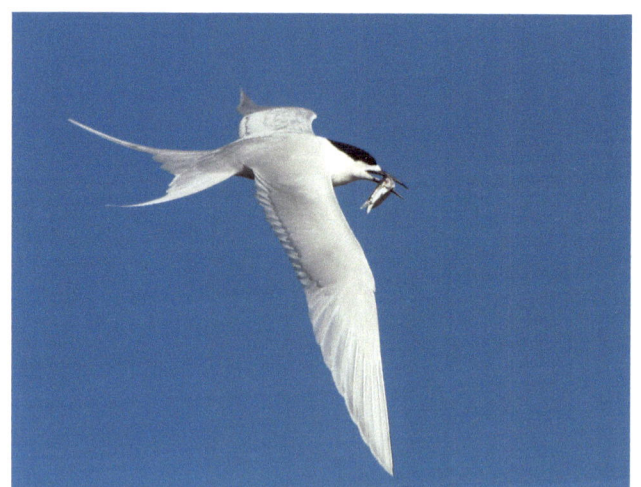

White-fronted tern showing a clear view of its wing. Thornton, Bay of Plenty. July.

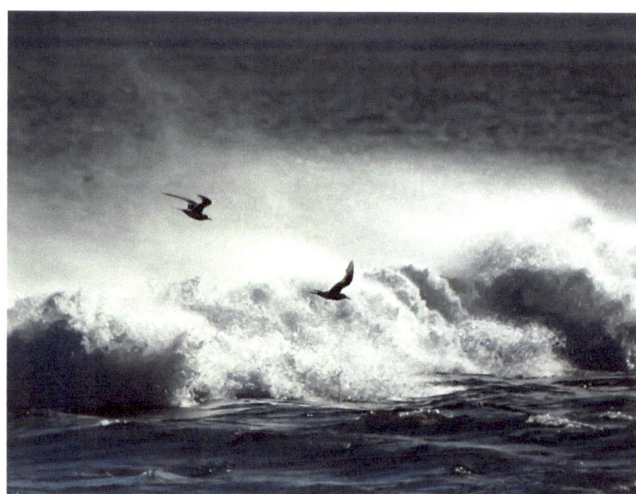

White-fronted terns in silhouette. Lake Ferry, Wairarapa. March.

36

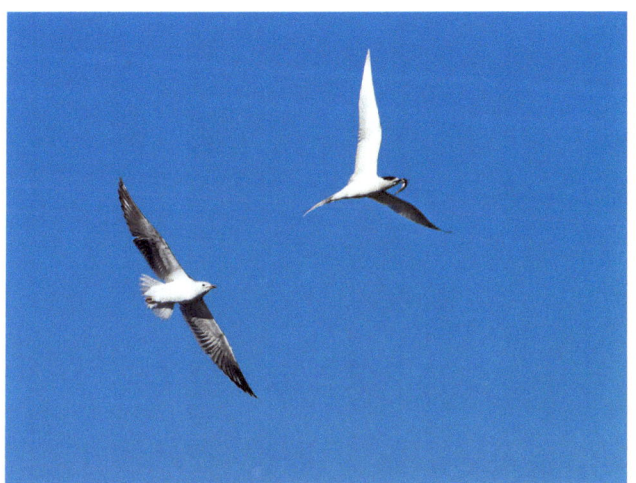

An opportunistic red-billed gull trying to steal the fish from the white-fronted tern. Thornton, Bay of Plenty. July.

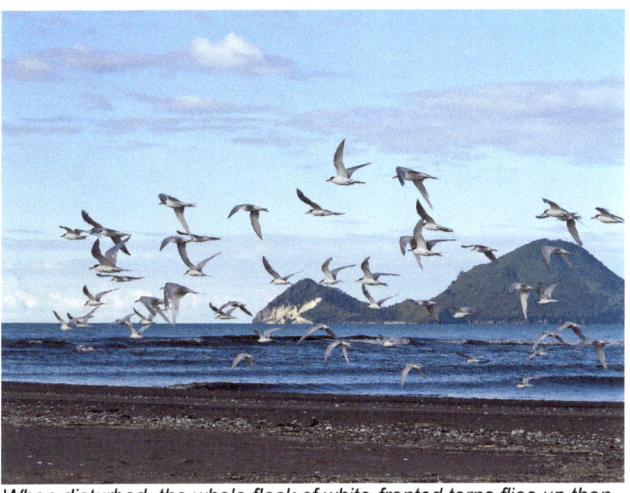

When disturbed, the whole flock of white-fronted terns flies up then lands again just a few metres away. Thornton, Bay of Plenty. March.

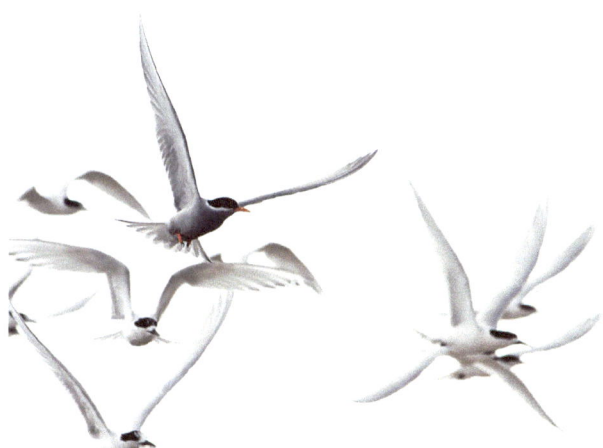

Single black-fronted tern with a flock of white-fronted terns. Note the fan shaped tail. Thornton, Bay of Plenty. July.

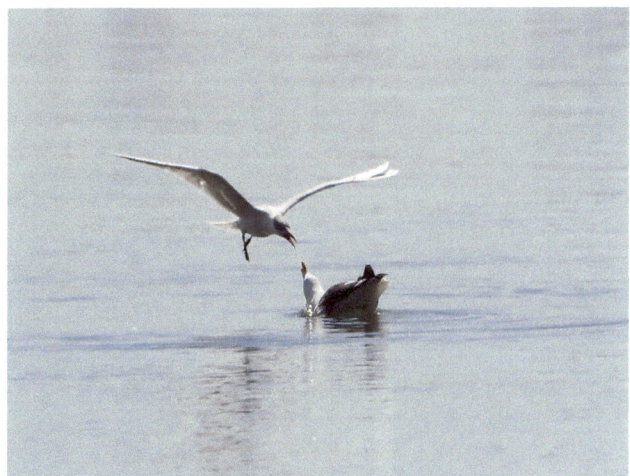

Caspian tern attacking a black-backed gull. The tern's mate was nearby on the water. This gull and another nearby were repeatedly attacked by the tern which harassed each of them in turn. Omokoroa, Tauranga Harbour. September.

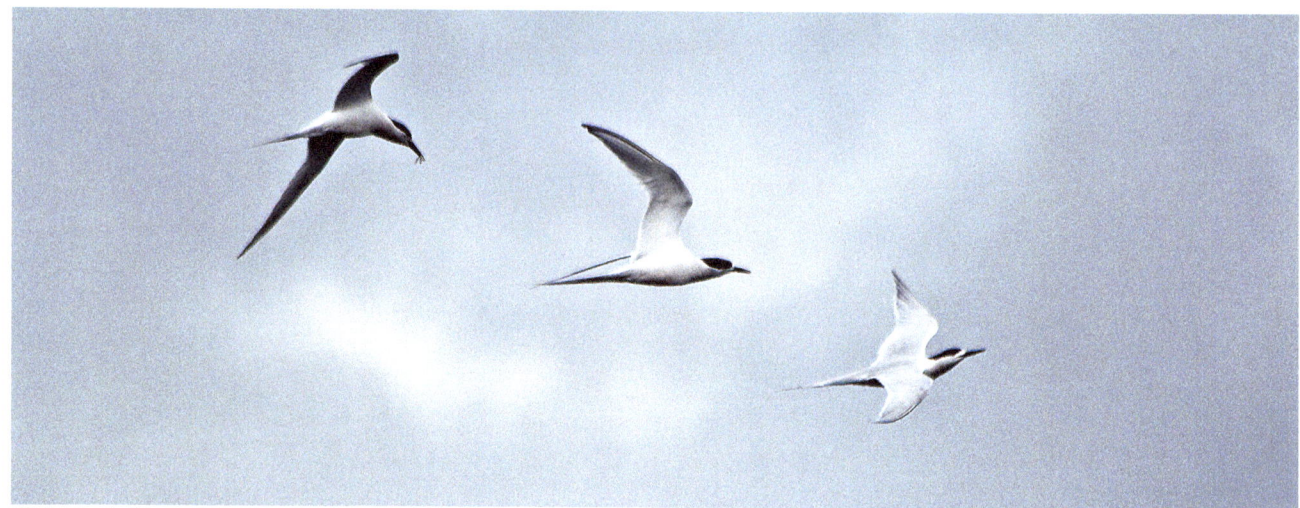

White-fronted terns flying together in a courtship display. The male is trying to attract the females by offering a fish. Tauranga Harbour. October.

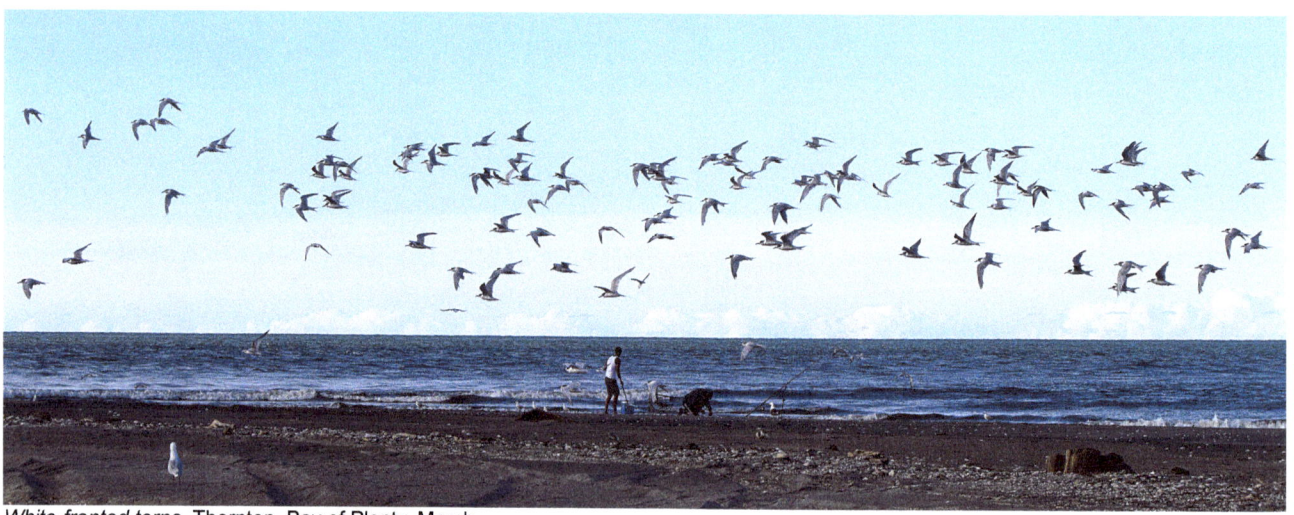

White-fronted terns. Thornton, Bay of Plenty. March.

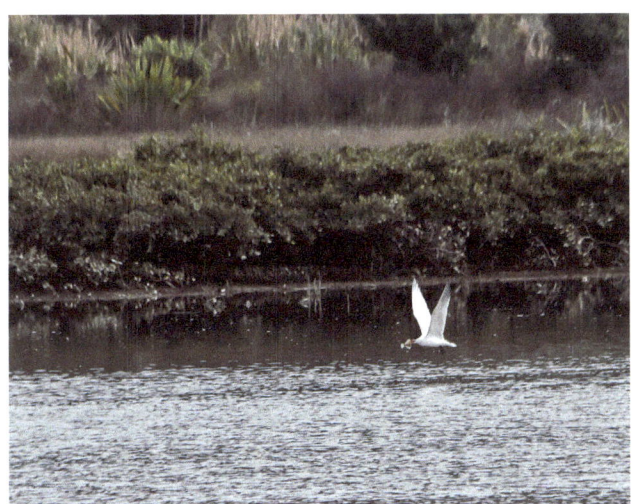

Caspian tern with a small flounder. Waikareao Estuary, Tauranga. August.

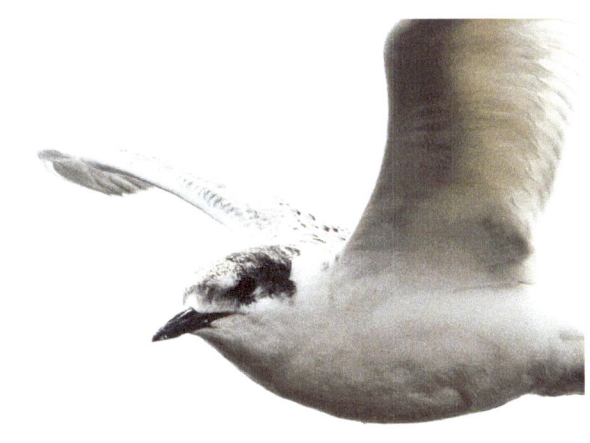

Juvenile white-fronted tern. Kapowairua, Far North. November.

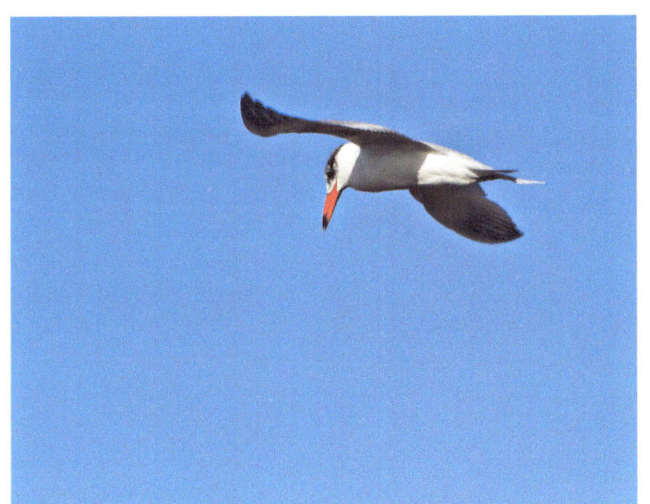

Caspian terns usually fly alone when fishing. The large bill will be pointed downwards looking for fish, making the bird easy to recognise in flight. When they see something, they hover for a moment before diving to catch it. Matata, Bay of Plenty. July.

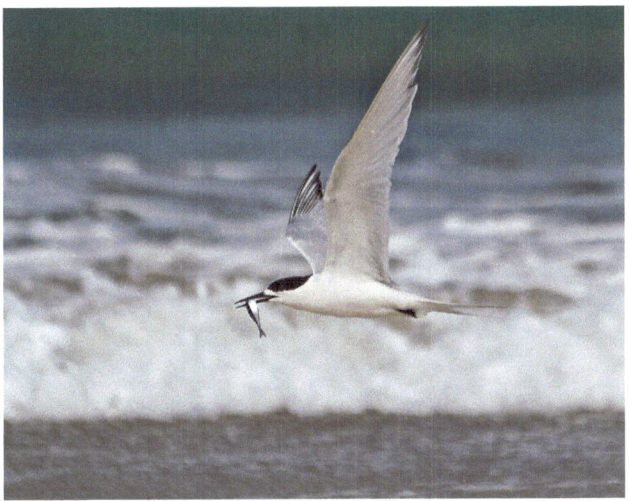

White-fronted tern. Kapowairua, Far North. November.

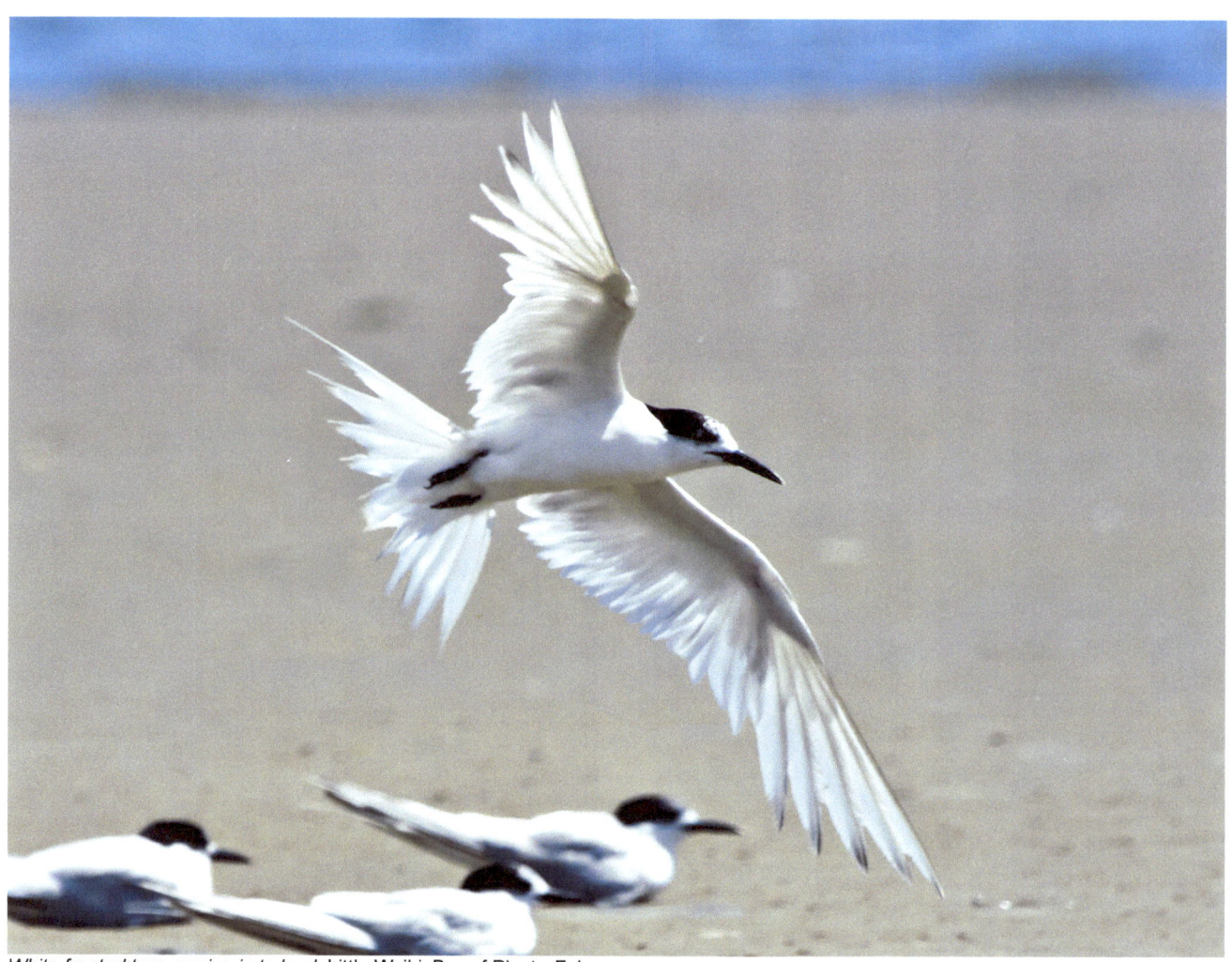

White fronted tern coming in to land. Little Waihi, Bay of Plenty. February.

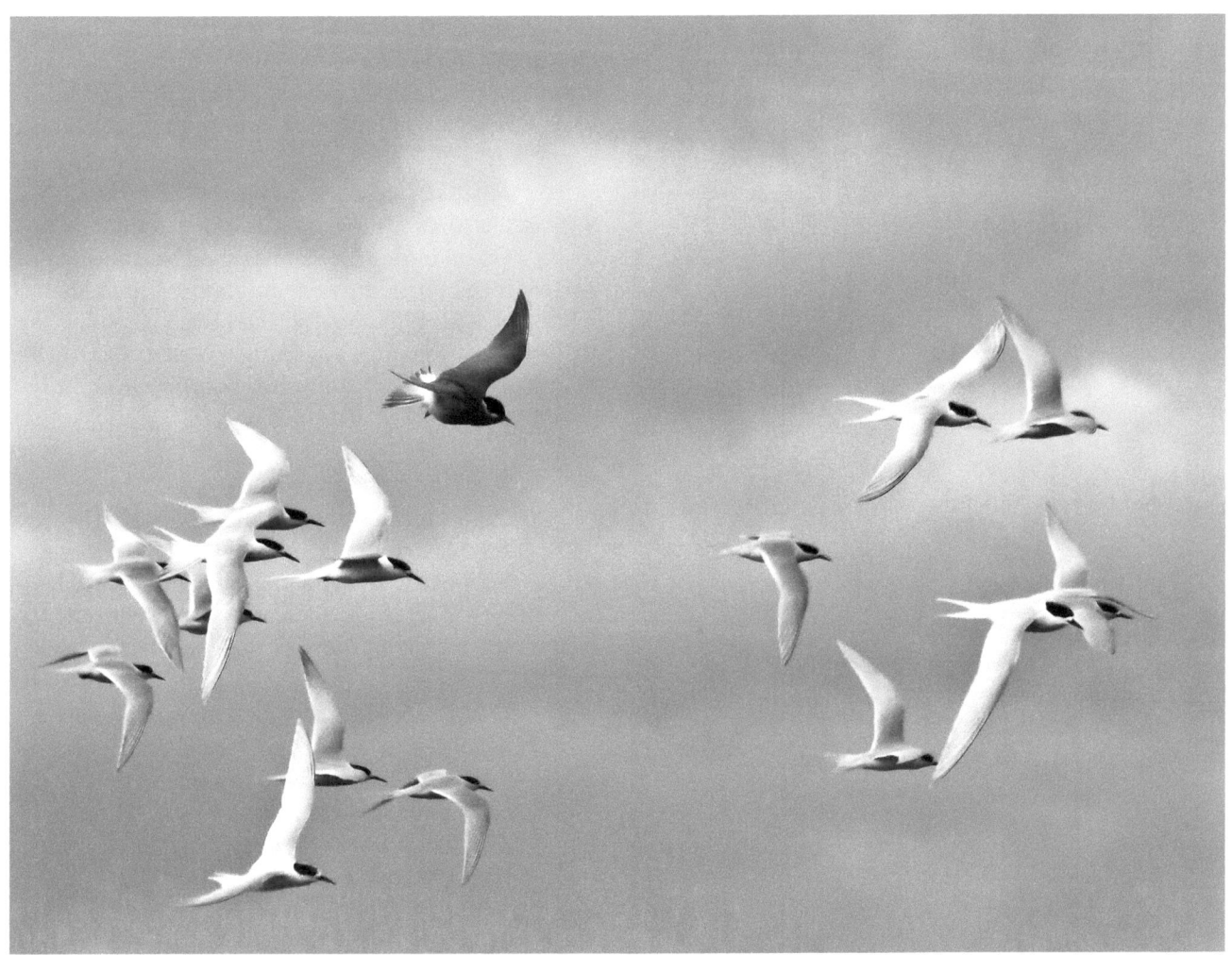

*A single black-fronted tern flying with a flock of white-fronted terns. Note the swallow shaped tails of the white-fronted terns.*Thornton, Bay of
Plenty. July.

OTHER TERNS

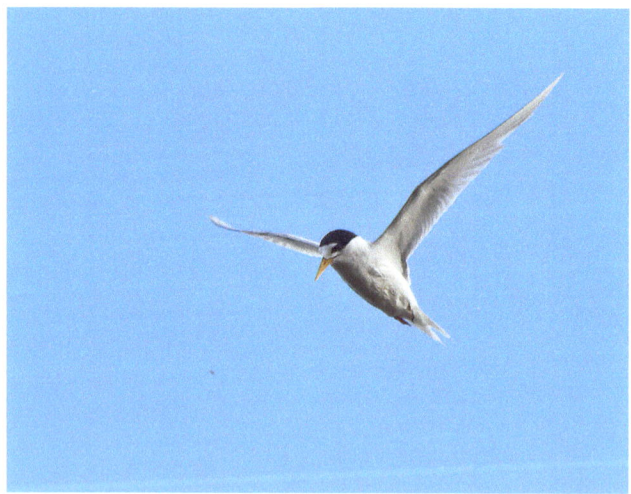

Fairy tern. Above and below Pakiri, Auckland. November.

A number of other terns may be seen occasionally in New Zealand. They are likely to be seen as a single bird or two in the company of white-fronted terns. It is always worth checking groups of terns for odd birds, some of which will look very like their companions.

- **Antarctic terns** (*Sterna vittata*) breed in the Antarctic and islands of the Southern Ocean during November and December. After breeding, many birds migrate to the southern coasts of South Africa and South America. Occasionally a migrating bird strays to New Zealand. Only a few have ever been sighted on the New Zealand mainland.

- **Arctic terns** (*Sterna paradisaea*) breed in the Arctic and surrounding area from May to July then migrate south to Antarctic regions. Very occasionally a migrating bird strays to New Zealand. Only a few have ever been sighted on the New Zealand mainland.

- **Common terns** (*Sterna hirundo*) breed in many countries in the northern hemisphere then migrate south to many southern hemisphere locations, usually excluding New Zealand. A few sightings of vagrants have been recorded here.

- **Eastern little terns** (*Sterna albifrons sinensis*) breed in Europe, Africa, Asia and northern Australia. Migratory stragglers are seen in New Zealand reasonably regularly.

- **Fairy terns** (*Sterna nereis davisae*) are New Zealand's most endangered endemic bird. Other forms of *Sterna nereis* exist in Australia and New Caledonia, but *Sterna nerei davisae* is unique to New Zealand. The fairy tern is the smallest tern and is now found in very low numbers at only a few nest sites north of Auckland. In the 1980s numbers were reduced to only three known pairs but they have now increased to about 40 birds. It is still severely endangered.

  Breeding and habits are fairly typical of terns. Breeding pairs may abandon nests that are disturbed so this should be avoided. After breeding a few birds migrate to other North Island locations but overall are rarely seen. Size 250mm.

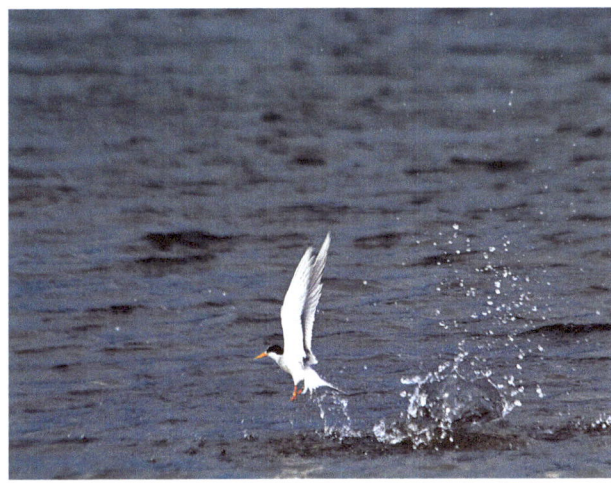

Fairy tern fishing over the river estuary. Above and below. Pakiri, Auckland. November.

- **Gull-billed terns** (*Sterna nilotica*) breed mainly in temperate zones of the northern hemisphere but also in some southern hemisphere areas. Birds migrate south and are occasionally seen in New Zealand.

- **Whiskered terns** (*Chlidonias hybrida*) breed in Africa, southern Europe, Asia and Australia. Vagrants are rarely seen in New Zealand.

- **White-winged black terns** (*Chlidonias leucopterus*) breed from eastern Europe through Asia and are seen in Australia. Stragglers are seen in New Zealand reasonably regularly.

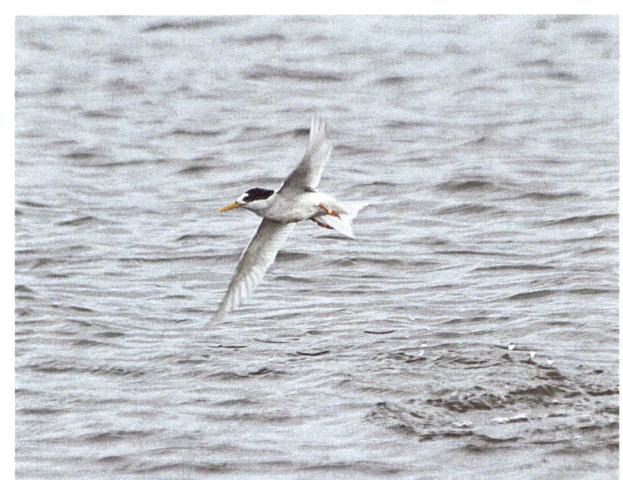

FURTHER INFORMATION

This is a small selection of the variety of books and other resources available to the person who is interested in learning more about these birds.

Arkins, A. & Doel, L. (2005). *Introducing New Zealand birds*. Auckland: Reed.

Buller, W. L. (1888). *A history of the birds of New Zealand*. London: Buller. Available online from http://www.nzetc.org/tm/scholarly/tei-BulBird.html.

Chambers. S. (1989). *Birds of New Zealand : locality guide*. Hamilton: Arun.

Chambers, S. (2007). *New Zealand birds : an identification guide*. Auckland: Reed.

Chudleigh, B. (2001). *Shorebirds of New Zealand : a photographic showcase*. Katikati: B. Chudleigh.

Crowe, A. & Gunson, D. (2001). *Which New Zealand bird?* Auckland: Penguin.

Guthrie-Smith, H. (1925). *Bird life on island and shore*. Edinburgh: William Blackwood and Sons. Available from http://www.nzetc.org/tm/scholarly/tei-GutLife.html.

Handbook of Australian, New Zealand & Antarctic birds. (Vols 1-7, 1990-2006) . Melbourne: Oxford University Press.

Hansen, K. (2006). *New Zealand fairy tern (Sterna nereis davisae) recovery plan, 2005–15*. Wellington: Department of Conservation. Available from http://www.doc.govt.nz/upload/documents/science-and-technical/tsrp57.pdf.

Heather, B. D. & Robertson, H. A. (2005). *The field guide to the birds of New Zealand*. Auckland: Viking.

International Union for Conservation of Nature. *IUCN red list of threatened species*. http://www.iucnredlist.org.

Medway, D. G. (2002). *The Reed field guide to common New Zealand shorebirds*. Auckland: Reed.

Medway, D. G. (2002). S*ea and shore birds of New Zealand*. Auckland: Reed.

Moon, G. (2002). *A photographic guide to birds of New Zealand*. Auckland: New Holland.

Moon, G. (1995). *Common birds in New Zealand 2*. Auckland: Reed.

Morris, R. & Ballance, A. (2006). *Beautiful birds of New Zealand*. Auckland: Random House.

New Zealand birds : nga manu o Aotearoa http://www.nzbirds.com/.

Royal Forest and Bird Protection Society of New Zealand. http://www.forestandbird.org.nz/.

Ornithological Society of New Zealand http://osnz.org.nz/.

Reader's Digest (1985). *Complete book of New Zealand birds*. Sydney: Reed Methuen.

Robertson, C. J. R., et al. (2007). *Atlas of bird distribution in New Zealand : 1999-2004*. Wellington: Ornithological Society of New Zealand.

www.ingramcontent.com/pod-product-compliance
Lightning Source LLC
Chambersburg PA
CBHW041516280526
45792CB00004B/1274